Helping our children talk

Helping our children talk

A guide for teachers of young or handicapped children

Hilda J. Meers

Longman   London and New York

Longman Group Limited
London and New York
Associated companies, branches and representatives
throughout the world

First published 1976
Second impression 1978

ISBN 0 582 25014.5 cased edition
ISBN 0 582 25010.2 paper edition

Library of Congress Cataloging in Publication Data

Meers, Hilda J
  Helping our children talk.

  (Longman early childhood education series)
  Bibliography: p. 147.
  Includes index.
  1. Children — Language. 2. Mentally handicapped children — Language.
  I. Title.
LB1139.L3M385 372.6 75-43561
ISBN 0-582-25014-5
ISBN 0-582-25010-2 pbk.

Printed in Great Britain by
T. & A. Constable Ltd, Edinburgh

Acknowledgements

We are grateful to the following for permission to reproduce copyright material:

The City of Birmingham Education Department for the examples of children's writing. We regret that we have been unable to trace the copyright holder of a *Yes–No Questions table* from *Child Language and Education* by C.B. Cazden and would appreciate any information that would enable us to do.

To those who supplied me with encouragement, advice, information, criticism, typing skill and black coffee, my sincere thanks.

iv

Contents

1

Helping the non-talking or language delayed child

Some years ago, a family moved into the vacant house two doors away from where we lived. Their children, aged six, five and four years, began to make friends with us. This family had recently arrived from Pakistan, and the two elder children, Asad and Ruby, had picked up some English. Anjum, aged four years, made no attempt to speak. It was a situation providing an opportunity to observe what would happen to a child encountering a language community different from his own.

Asad and Ruby had open happy expressions and beaming smiles. Anjum was frowning and gloomy. When his brother and sister came to play, he would come too, select a few cars from the toys available, and silently play in a corner by himself. One day I asked Ruby if Anjum understood English. While she replied: 'Some he do, some he don't', Anjum vigorously shook his head in denial. I asked if he spoke Pakistani, and was told that he did, but not English. 'Anjum, do you understand me?' I asked. His head shook more vigorously than ever. 'Yes he do' insisted Ruby. But Anjum maintained his silence.

Late that night, long after the children had gone home, there was a knock on the door. There stood Anjum. He held out to me a small toy (evidently it had been taken home by mistake) which he had been sent to return. 'Eeyah' said Anjum. After a moment of stupefaction I realized he had not spoken Pakistani. It was his first English phrase; 'Here you are,' rendered in Brummagem dialect.

In the days that followed, his indistinct 'jargon' sentences became clearly enunciated; in a few weeks he could carry on conversations. With these achievements a remarkable change came over him. The characteristic frown was replaced by a cheeky grin, the silence by voluble comment.

He lost a certain very expressive look with which he used to turn his head from side to side to show displeasure. He greeted strange adults with a confident 'Hello', and played with other children on a basis of equality. He began to greet me with a typically British need to comment on the weather: 'It's warm today, isn't it?'.

Acquiring the language of the community he lived in made a great difference to the kind of life Anjum could lead. As a process, acquiring language is something we all go through; because it is usual we are inclined to take it for granted. It is only when something goes wrong somewhere that we realize how pervasive are the effects of language, how hampered we are if language skills are stunted. Teachers often express themselves as being at a loss, not knowing how to deal with the situation of children whose language is different, inadequate or completely lacking. Since we ourselves have not had the school experience of being systematically taught to listen, to understand language and to speak it, this reaction is understandable.

Any attempt to help teachers in this situation has to take into account our notion of what language is, and how it is acquired. I treat it as inseperable from our notion of how we act, perceive, think, feel and know. A part of this knowing is knowing who one is as a person, what are the rules of living, where one fits in the family and wider society.

Learning to understand what someone else says and to express oneself in spoken language, are stages of a process peculiar to human beings. Chomsky advanced the notion that it requires the knowledge, at a deep level of the mind, of ways in which types of rules are used on strings of word symbols. This underlying grammar transforms the interconnected words by rewriting them into what our conscious mind recognizes as sentences. This enables us to produce new and original sentence forms, as well as previously heard ones. The three factors of rules, changes to these rules, and the creative qualities of the system are combined in the phrase 'generative transformational grammar'. Since the advent of this hypothesis of generative transformational grammar, this question of how young children acquire their native language and how they learn to use it creatively, has been the subject of much research. Not only has research increased quantitatively, its quality is more subtle and complex, reflecting our new acknowledgement of language's complexity and of its inseparability from the social setting in which it occurs. The nature of processes involved in human cognitive functioning has also had to be rethought. As Greene (1972) puts it:

. . . Chomsky's demonstration of the need for rules to produce language has had an important effect on the analysis of many cognitive, perceptual and even motor skills. Reversing the claim that even such complex skills as verbal behaviour can be explained in terms of peripheral chains of stimulus-response associations Miller, Galanter and Pribram take the opposite position that virtually all behaviour needs to be centrally planned . . . (p 19)

I want to show how we may attempt to apply our still limited but growing knowledge to the task of helping children whose disabilities (possibly connected with difficulty in the central planning of their behaviour) present more or less intractable learning problems. These are children who, at five plus, cannot or do not talk; whose language is delayed or different; or who have such poor articulation of words and sentences that conversation is much restricted. These are the kind of problems which teachers in reception or nursery classes in ESN (M) and ESN (S) schools have to deal with, among the other disabilities of their pupils.

Since the assessment procedures which have led to the child's classification (as ESN (M) and ESN (S)) do not give a clear indication to the teacher of a child's specific language difficulty, classroom procedures for deciding types of language experiences needed by each child have to be worked out. These are then continued or modified in the light of on-going evaluation of their success. The approach which I outline here is necessarily tentative; we still have a great deal to learn about how children acquire thinking and language skills in the course of social interaction. All that I can lay claim for it is that its application, with children in an educational priority area who have a wide range of disabilities, has brought encouraging results.

Assessment
Teachers need an understanding of the processes of language acquisition to help them develop their own insights, sharpen their own perceptual awareness of language. Bringing together with this their knowledge from a variety of other fields, the teacher and other members of staff must:

1 Build up a sufficiently warm and supportive relationship with the child. We need to distinguish this from mawkishness. Interaction and encouragement are necessary as a trigger to language potential, even more so than other forms of stimulation in the environment (Sampson, 1958). In an interesting discussion, Danziger (1971) has pointed out that the child should not be regarded as the passive recipient of warmth (or hostility), but as also producing it by his actions. It is a question of what results from a reciprocal web of relationships. Seen in this way, the warmth which parent or teacher shows to the child is a measure of their success in meeting the child's needs as expressed by his demands. Functionally, it is seen as providing a suitable personal model for the child to learn from by observation (p 65).

2 Build up a store of information, using social and specialist services as necessary, about:
   a the child's family and home background. What are the general

3

circumstances, atmosphere and attitudes like? What is the child's position in the family, and how closely are his siblings spaced? Is there a history of hospitalization or other separation experiences? At what age did these occur and for how long? More important, how did he react to these?

b Physical factors. Are there any known disabilities, or any suspected through observation? What is known about the child's hearing and sight? (The importance of good vision for language is more easily overlooked than the need for good hearing.) Is nutrition thought to have been and to be good? Does the child get enough sleep? Was there delay or deviance in passing 'motor milestones'? Did the child suck well? Can he lick and chew? Is he clumsy? From what causes? What illnesses has he had, and at what age?

c Social and emotional factors. Is he unduly attention-seeking, withdrawn, shy, timid, aggressive or anxious? In what circumstances does he show these traits? How does he relate to other children? to adults? Is his behaviour variable in school? If so, when and why? Is he much the same at school and at home?

d Cognitive factors. Curiosity, attention, remembering, anticipation, planning, integration of actions, integration of perceptions. Can he classify, and at what level? What 'mistakes' does he make in classifying? Is he lethargic or spontaneous? What is his level of play – does he pretend? Can he follow simple instructions in context? – out of context? Has he functionally useful concepts of up/down, bigger than/smaller than, more/less, before/after etc.?

e Non-verbal responses. Does he make eye contact, watch, look interested, smile, laugh, respond to facial expression and gesture? Does he gesture and mime simple actions? Does he join in singing? Does he pull at or tap adults to get attention, show what he wants? Does he accompany this with grunts? Does he cry, shriek or hit to show what he wants (or doesn't want)? Does he do what the other children do?

Diagnosis and Treatment

The teacher's informed observation and the pooling of other information, leads to a tentative formulation, a decision about why the child doesn't speak; to proposed treatment based on this; and then to evaluation leading to a continuation or modification of the approach being followed. The main types of problem, listed below as separate dysfunctions, are usually met with as overlapping or interrelated conditions.

1 The child has defects of hearing and/or sight, needing:

a proper use and maintenance of existing aids.

b referral to specialist agencies for assessment and provision of aids, with training in using these.

c provision of a nursery/infant type school programme while these measures are taken and their effect assessed.

2 The child has apparently normal or near-normal auditory and visual perception, but he doesn't understand what language is about. He needs:

a to learn to bring attention to the task of listening.

b to learn to discriminate environmental sounds.

c to learn to discriminate words from sounds, and to select these for auditory attention.

d to discover that his own sounds can alter his environment for the better.

e the stimulation and experiences of a nursery school type programme.

3 He understands aspects of language, but cannot produce a spoken response. He needs:

a attention to physical factors leading to readiness of speech organs and muscles.

b adults who use clear, short, complete and appropriate sentences as a model for the child's speech.

c adults who supply more complex language samples through rhymes, stories, singing games, songs, jokes, conversational exchanges. Conversations between adults is particularly important for children from one-parent or immigrant families.

d adults who use a multi-sensory structured approach to develop expressive responses (Molloy, 1965) through spaced practice.

e child models who will increase his motivation to join in play and conversations.

f a nursery school type programme.

4 He understands language as used for simple instructions and requests, produces naming words as labels (or sounds which approximate to these). He needs:

a adults who understand, approve of, repeat, expand, comment on and reply to what he tries to say.

b a growing range of stories, nursery rhymes, finger-play rhymes and songs, to extend his awareness of intonational patterns and of language structures, and to reveal to him the pleasure that language gives.

c experiences and outings which enlarge his labelling activities, providing the basis for a rich vocabulary.

d a nursery school type programme.

5 He has a good understanding of language structures, with sufficient cognitive development to demonstrate this comprehension, but has marked articulatory defects which inhibit his attempts to converse. He needs:

a to build up confidence through success experiences.

b to continue to work on the comprehension of increasingly difficult language structures.

c a wide range of structured practice, in a one-to-one situation with the teacher, in the form of the free production and repetition of short sentences of increasing structural difficulty, in ways which will transfer to daily use (Meers, 1972).

d infilling of gaps in his knowledge resulting from his poor and late talking.

6 He understands language, is able but unwilling to speak, is moderately but not too severely disturbed. He needs:

a team application of behaviour modification methods, to get him to make verbal requests and responses.

b individual practice with part/whole of specific language programmes, to make up for his previous lack of practice.

c a nursery/infant type school programme.

7 He protects himself from what he conceives of as a threatening environment by not listening or speaking, though he is at times able to do both. He needs:

a a reduction of stress and anxiety.

b a gradual approach to him by an adult who is willing to accept the level which he is at, behaviourally, and in his motivation (Hewett, 1964).

c a long-term programme aimed at satisfying his basic needs, increasing the social interactions he can tolerate.

d provision of non-verbal communicative symbolic forms, e.g. drawing, music, therapeutic play, dance-drama, through which he can make a statement of his problems and find step-by-step solutions to them (Griffiths, 1935).

e progression from motivation at the level of primary extrinsic rewards to abstract and intrinsic rewards.

f an improved self-image; when the child can accept himself as a person, he can bear to name himself as 'I'.

Evaluation

Objective evaluation of the suitability of the devised programme is complicated by the fact that observed progress will be different for each child, depending upon his age, abilities, attitudes, previous experiences. A child from a very unstimulating home should make rapid advances, a multi-handicapped child is likely to progress at a slower rate, but continue at this rate for a longer period of time. Comparisons with normally learning three to five-year-olds may be helpful for evaluation.

Research is reported by Brannon with children of nursery-school age, which used written sounds and tapes of this age group's spontaneous speech in the course of free play, and with 26 sentence types. His study tends to confirm that normally children seem to acquire syntactic rules in this order: phrase structure, simple transformations, generalized transformations. The four-year-olds used significantly more transformations than three-year-olds, and they expanded their sentences much more (Brannon, 1968). When one listens to children of this age conversing together, a rivalry pattern may occur: **1** statement, **2** elaborated reply, **3** further statement repeating elements of first statement but adding new information etc., in which each child tries to outdo the other, as the opening remark is partially repeated but changed, as the discourse moves back and forward between them. Take these three-year-olds on a bus trip.

Joanne: I'm going to get married.

Rajel: I'm going to marry my boy friend.

Joanne: You know who's going to marry me — my boy friend.

This flow continued for three minutes. By this time Joanne had progressed to new subject matter and a confidently sustained sentence: 'We're going to have a baby brother when we move to our new house — are you?' Rajel contented herself with replying 'We're going to have a nice house, we're moving.' The subject then changed.

Both children lived in and attended school in an educational priority area. Their talk seems to be transitional between a genuine interchange and parallel monologues, echoing the associative type of play which is so common at this age, when children play alongside each other, may even appear to be playing together, but are not yet engaged in truly co-operative play (Cass, 1971).

Evaluation of progress in language has to take into account complexity and length of sentence; tone and style of interaction; its suitability to the occasion; whether or not there is in it a recognition of the relative status of the participants, the ability to stop as well as start a conversation, to listen when it is one's turn to listen. These skills, dependent largely on many opportunities for practice, are needed if a natural sounding use of language is to be made possible. Besides this, there is the child's own attitudes to his growing skills. As Cratty and Martin (1971) have pointed out, it is possible for children's performance scores to improve significantly yet the child's feelings about his performance not to do so (p 159–160). We need to check on how the child thinks he is getting on.

Besides questions aimed at seeing if the programme is as good as we can make it, we have also to assess if it is being put over as efficiently and economically as possible. There is a level of activity or arousal which we need to aim at in order to get and keep the child's attention on what we want him to learn. This level will be affected by fatigue, by hunger, by anxiety, fear of failure in the task, temperature, weather conditions, outside distractions. Some tense, hyperactive or distractable children will be helped by learning how to relax their muscles. To do this they have to learn to recognize when they are tense and know what to do about it. Games can suggest contrasts: walking like a clockwork toy, wobbling like a jelly etc., specific practice in stiffening muscles, then making them loose, makes the aim clearer to the child. These are just some of the ways in which a difficult concept can be experienced. When a child has learned to hear the difference between a glockenspiel resonating correctly after being struck with a loose wrist movement, and the sound produced when a stiffly held beater stops the tone, he can hear whether or not his wrist is relaxed.

Slow movement is more difficult for any young child than quick movement, but if the child can be cued by rhythmic beats he can gradually learn the control he needs. Increasing the span of attention can be achieved through transfer from creative activities such as painting, or soothing ones such as water play, which often provide a level of absorption not often seen in the distractable child. Another method is to add on new elements to a task the child performs well but briefly. This can be done not only with motor tasks, but in games in which instructions are given. An increase in the length of the message which has to be acted on can go like this: first version, 'Go to the door and sit down', later version, 'Go to the door, touch it, walk all the way round the room, sit down.' Here again, we should remember to let the child know how much he has improved.

The timing of any programme should consider the child's pattern of wakefulness. Usually we aim for morning teaching, but a fatigued child who went to bed late may not be at optimal arousal until late in the morning, a child who is hungry will need food before we give him food for thought. Spaced practice, short periods of concentration with time in between for what has been learned to sink in and be incorporated into previous patterns of experience, is known to be more effective than practice given in infrequent large lumps. Since there is never enough time in a school day to teach all that one plans to teach, economy should be practised in that methods used should be multi-purpose. For example, a game in which increasingly long instructions have to be translated into action by the child, while primarily planned as extension of attention span, also develops sequencing ability and remembering. If the child has to repeat the teacher's instructions he is practising expressive language and learning to use it to mediate a task. If he is then asked to repeat the message after he has completed it, he is learning to separate the word from its referent. By playing the game in a group situation where other children watch and comment on his performance, he is learning to tolerate social stress without too great an adverse effect on his performance. The other children in the group are learning to take turns and to moderate their comments in consideration for the feelings of the child who is acting out the instructions. Since the learning situation is not restricted to the children, the teacher is also learning, both to analyse simple activities in this way, to watch for reactions, notice pacing, level of interest, and when and how to make transitions to other activities just before the children's interest starts to flag, and plan for follow-up work.

Since we are teaching in ways which we hope will facilitate transfer, building bridges from experiences to similar experiences, we should be able to make some assessment of the helpfulness of our language teaching programme by looking at its effect on the child's functioning in related but separate areas. Thus it is valid to ask the following questions. Is the child showing overall improvement in:

1 attitudes – confidence, happiness, spontaneity, friendships? Has his level of motivation changed?

2 abilities – have gross and fine motor skills and co-ordination improved? Visual perception and visuo-motor skills? Have auditory perception and discrimination developed? Auditory sequencing and remembering? Has he learned more of how to attend, what to attend to? Has his ability to classify developed? Can he recognize shapes by touch? Can he distinguish the quality of notes made by different musical instruments when these are only heard? Has his level of play moved from simple manipulation of objects to integrated schemes involving imagery? Has the gap between his language competence and his performance narrowed? Has he gained in knowledge of simple concepts?

The answers to these and similar questions may suggest that modifications to the child's language programme should be made. In deciding how to modify, further suggested questions are:

1 Is he bored because it's too easy for him – in whole or in part?

2 Is he anxious because it's too difficult for him – in whole or in part?

3 Is he too pre-occupied with his own problems to be mentally available to us? What bridges can we devise between such a child's experience and our own?

4 Has the child now moved on to a higher stage in motivation?

5 Has the child now moved on to a new stage in language acquisition?

6 Is he able to use gains made in situations of increasing social complexity? i.e. to withstand pressure from any group which may criticize his performance.

To illustrate how this general approach is made more specific, I will expand **3** above (see also p 5) to show what we do with a child who understands a conversational exchange on a simple level but who is without expressive language.

It would be desirable (although unrealistic to expect it) to have the advice of a speech therapist about the normality or deformation of the child's nose, throat and mouth (see Renfrew, 1972). As it is, we can get the child (or note his inability) to imitate tongue movements, teach him to suck his milk through a straw, observe his chewing at dinnertime, play games such as blowing a paper boat across the water, blowing bubbles through a straw in soapy water, blowing a ping-pong ball across a table. (Concepts of light/heavy can come in here.) At story time, he can imitate our yawning, pretend to lick lollipops and chew pretend toffees. Touch, taste and smell can all be utilized and refined. Group activity can be blended with individual practice using objects whose names start with a sound which can be seen and felt as well as heard, i.e. 'b', 'p', 'm' and 'ch'. Molloy suggests using these toys: a ball, a baby, a bell, a boat, a bus, in that order; first using these when the child needs to gain understanding of what language is for, and proceeding by the carefully graded stages of a multi-sensory approach which thus brings maximum information to the child.

Feelings are very much the trail breaker in developing spoken language (Chaloner, 1963). Group games play an important part, e.g. contrasting whispering with shouting in *Jack in the Box* and *Pop goes the weasel*. (The first three lines of this are whispered, the last shouted as loudly as possible. De-climaxing techniques are needed after this.) We use animal sounds occurring in stories to get noise from a child in a group situation, as this does not make him feel self-conscious. Miming simple actions and following instructions in sequence come in the old favourite, *Here we go round the Mulberry Bush*, or in newly devised songs.

Discriminating sounds can also be taught in a variety of group situations, such as listening to tapes of environmental sounds and acting out the situations they suggest. The Carl Orff music teaching scheme is useful since its approach hinges on the child extracting sound from his own environment and experiencing it as such. Experience becomes patterned: e.g. handclaps to the rhythms of people's names; repeating a clapped pattern, first with the teacher and then, after much practice, from memory; the grouping of familiar objects into categories for rhythmic speaking; the use of the interval of the natural call in a question-and-answer dialogue which stabilizes the voice. The notions of high and low, up and down, can be taught in ways which help with body image and awareness, through their physical representation. Attention can be drawn to the intonational patterns which through their 'tune' help to convey the meaning of a sentence, in situations which are intrinsically interesting to the child: they concern his experience. The carrying out of instructions requires further development of the child's attentional and listening techniques, and through learning to stop at a signal, a child learns to inhibit his own response. Translating the heard sounds of a name into a pattern of handclaps gives practice in the art of transferring sensations experienced through one channel, hearing, into a different sense mode, the physical act of hand-clapping. It is an example of the kind of skill involved in cross-modal coding. It will be needed when the stage of reading is reached; for the visual experience of words on the page has to be turned mentally into sounds.

In the kind of activities which are suited to this pre-reading stage, the later needs are being considered and prepared for as the thinking skills of cross-modal coding, as well as sequencing and categorizing are being painlessly developed. For the free experimentation with musical sound which is also needed, I provide a glockenspiel which the children play at most times, with the sole proviso that they use the beaters correctly to produce a pleasant tone. When we sing, the non-talkers frequently enjoy a wordless attempt at the tune.

Where rhythmic movement, and the ability to imitate gesture need to be developed, the ability to duplicate a pattern in movement may be helped by a multi-sensory presentation. Cratty describes Robin's method in these terms:

Easiest are reactions to even tempos involving both visual and auditory stimuli presented at the same time. The vivid flag waving indigenous to the splendid programme outlined by Robins, for example, can be expected to elicit the attention of a severely retarded child who is often out of contact with his environment. The flags are heard rippling as they are moved rapidly, at the same time, their bright colours and their movements tend to hold his attention. Thus, he may begin, slowly at first, to react to this type of intense stimuli entering his consciousness through several sensory 'channels' at the same time. (Cratty and Martin, p 153)

Other times when sounds can be elicited freely are: in the swimming baths, where the general background of noise, and the freedom of splashing in the water, encourage an uninhibited response; on bus trips, outings etc. (which should be many and varied). The first two clearly enunciated words the child produces are likely to be swear words: another tribute to the power of feeling.

So we come to know that the child can produce sounds, and possibly words, in some circumstances. Probably the child will then have a 'naming' stage in which he pulls at adults, at the same time pointing to the object or person he wants to hear named. Maybe he will also say 'da' in an attempt to enquire 'What's that?' The teacher's response takes two forms.

1 'That's . . .' This treats the child's action as a request for information, which is then supplied to him.

2 'Yes, that's right, that's . . .' This treats the child's action as a request for confirmation of what he thinks he knows from past experience: **a** that everything has its own name, and **b** that the name of this thing is '. . .'.

The child becomes more confident in attempting to name things and more able to do so, as the confirming adult accepts his attempt, crowning it with success. No systematic attempt is made at this stage to improve the child's articulation, as there is some danger of inhibiting his response, or of making him self-conscious about the imperfection of his efforts. The child will speak more clearly with practice anyway, and gets this through his pleasure in repeating adult's words and phrases.

It is now that parents often complain that their previously 'good' child is 'naughty' and wilful at home. We tell them that this is a good sign as the child is passing through a natural developmental stage. I consider the child is now becoming more aware of the 'rules' for living, and that much of his 'mischievous' behaviour is an attempt to discover what these rules are (Kagan, 1971). We also advise parents to turn a deaf ear to their child's swearing; a form of behaviour, however, usually exhibited in situations where it will cause maximum embarrassment to the adults concerned, making this advice the more difficult to follow.

The child of six to seven may well indicate at the following stage of his language development that he is not at all the same as the two-year-old learning to speak. For when he at last starts to put words together in simple sentences, he may not need to go through forms of primitive grammar. From labelling, he goes straight into the occasional 'What are those?' or 'I'll tell Mummy!'

The interacting teacher-model is providing language examples which are simple, brief and clear. The aim is to:

1 Demonstrate understanding of what the child tries to say.

2 Repeat what the child tries to say.

3 Repeat in expanded form what the child tries to say.

4 Approve what the child tries to say on the basis of its truth rather than its correctness, e.g. if a child says, 'Da tain', the reply might be 'Yes, that's right, that's a train,' but if, in the same circumstances, the child remarked, 'That is a bus', the reply would be, 'No, it's not, it's a train.'

5 Provide information to correct the notion which the child has tried to express, e.g. 'Doggy bite me!' – 'No he won't, he's only playing.'

6 Reply to what the child tries to say, in a series of lengthening conversational exchanges.

7 Provide an easy form of question through which the child can clarify what he tries to say, e.g. if he says 'I want a . . .', the teacher, with rising tone at the end, replies, 'You want a what?' Thus the child has only to make the effort to clarify the crucial word, instead of going through the whole thing. It can also be asked humorously, avoiding tensions and frustrations in the child, encouraging him to try again.

Children who have had many failure experiences at an early stage of language development, and who are reluctant to verbalize for that reason, are among those likely to enjoy and respond to the approach developed by Barnes, where the children copy body positions, actions and commands, first through the teacher's use of puppets, then with line drawings as a model, then from the child's movement response to a verbal one also. Then the ability to follow instructions without a picture clue is tested. The sequence is thus:

1 The language of the body.

2 The language of bodily movement.

3 The language of bodily position and direction of movement.

4 The language of spatial relationships.

5 The language of commands.

In addition to simple statements which the child can use directly as models, the teacher should provide more complex language structures, using in her talk with children and with other adults a range of stories, nursery rhymes, finger-plays, poems, songs, as a preparation for the next stages, and for the fun of it.

The additional need for the child to hear exchanges, discussions, verbal negotiations between adults, has to be kept in mind where in a one-parent situation the child does not have the opportunity to observe how adults go about resolving interpersonal situations through language use. For the child of immigrant parents it is important, because if he only hears this type of interchange in another language or dialect, he is limited in the range of uses to which he can put the English he is learning at school.

Language jokes and nonsense have their place in developing thinking. As Chukovsky (1963) has pointed out, the concept is clarified and defined by what it is not, and mastery is shown by the ability to use it in play forms. And we must realize that language has other, possibly more important, functions for the child than merely its use as a conceptual tool.

Halliday (1969) has pointed out the functional diversity and extent of language influence, beginning as it does through the form which language gives to child-adult interactions which begin at birth, mediating every aspect of his experience. Halliday suggests seven models of language which a child should have internalized by the age of five:

1 Instrumental – language can be used to get things done. It serves the expression of material needs through 'I want' indications.

2 Regulatory – this is how others use it as a means of exercising control over the child, and in turn is used by the child in relations with other children; it is elaborated into rules.

3 Interactional – the use of language in the interaction of the self with others can be both complex and subtle, including such feats as defining and consolidating the group; who can play and who can't, with all that this involves.

4 Personal – through this the child becomes aware of his own individuality, and realizes his personal identity. This in turn helps him to separate himself out from his environment, leading him to a more objective sense of himself compared to others.

5 Heuristic – finding out about reality, understanding how to use questions and answers for this purpose.

6 Imaginative – language play and pretending of all kinds.

7 Representational – as a means of communication through propositions expressed by the child, which relate to the real world of events and people.

Although our language-delayed child cannot yet use language in all these ways, we need to be aware that these are some of the goals that we are working towards for him. We can use the child's natural motivation in helping things on. For instance, children are strongly motivated by their desire to join in play with friends who can talk, so plenty of opportunity for 'house' play, and dramatic play of all kinds is called for. This is also important for the development of imagery indicating memory and symbolism antecedent to symbolism as used in language (Piaget, 1971). This is also emphasized in the thoughtful approach of Minuchin and Biber (1968) to the teaching of pre-school disadvantaged children. Here, pre-verbal communication and the development of symbolic play are seen as necessary stages preceding and supplementing specific language work. The teacher has to be deeply aware of what she is doing. She should neither force language on the child before relationships are made, nor present language in situations which give it little meaning. Language is offered to the child as a problem-solving tool in a situation which has rich emotional meaning for him. Consolidation of language in the context of the child's activities aims to provide language which can be and is used by the child.

It is a highly skilled approach, for the structure here is in the mind of the teacher, and has to be applied with imagination, ingenuity and, I feel, an inherent respect for the child as an individual.

Once the child is talking, he may make longer, more sustained remarks in talk which he has initiated with other children (or they with him), than in teacher-initiated conversation. He will also strive to become more intelligible to other children. (The balance of talkers to non-talkers within a class is thus of some importance.)

A programme to enlarge experience in and out of the classroom, and adults who make the most of the language possibilities which arise, gives the children a broader base of knowledge, opportunities to compare and contrast, and often triggers off fluent spontaneous comment, as well as enlarging the vocabulary. This type of teaching contrasts with but does not exclude the materials which have been expensively (though not aesthetically) packaged as the Peabody Kit; this collocation of ideas does in fact bring together many nursery/infant activities. Similarly much remediation based (rather superficially) on I.T.P.A. (The Illinois Test of Psycholinguistic Ability); this is the kind of thing that we infant teachers do almost as naturally as breathing (Hart, Karnes etc.).

One of the more difficult decisions which has to be made is whether a child would or would not benefit from part/whole of one or several of the 'structured' language programmes referred to in describing how the non-talker may be moved into the talking stage. The way 'perceptual and memory limitations interact with grammatical and notional aspects of the task' (Clay, 1971 p 34) have a bearing on this, connecting with many imponderable nuances based on the child's thinking and affective styles. I select three cases as illustrations of what I look and listen for.

Evelyn was admitted to ESN (M) school at five, reported to be generally backward, and markedly so in language development. Informed observation amended this picture, as a number of mild handicaps were noticed. Stance and gait suggested very slight spasticity. A visual problem, possibly restricted visual field, became apparent. A slight wry neck might be related to efforts to see better by altered posture. Her poor balance – she was constantly falling down or being accidentally knocked over by other children – led her to restrict experience needed for spatial relationships and gross motor control. Lack of this fine motor control, in part due to few opportunities in a not very stimulating home, plus her visual difficulties, discouraged her from attempting to develop skills. She could not hold a pencil well enough to make a mark with it, nor work a pair of scissors. She had no notion of direction. Her monosyllabic speech, with babyish articulation, reflected her attitude to herself.

The total effect of this range of difficulties was to lower drastically her level of attainment, frustrate her intentions, give Evelyn a misleading picture of herself, obscure her possible rate of learning and limit her social interactions with other children. Her school attendance suffered too, for Mum understandably kept her at home after her frequent falls. A variety of practice aimed at improving her balance included a specially made balance board, much encouragement to climb on, swing from and generally experiment on the climbing apparatus, and so on. The subsequent improvements were themselves valuable, but I believe less so than Evelyn's realization that 1 her problems were recognized by the teachers 2 that they were accepted, and 3 that they were dealt with. This was achieved by taking her into our confidence about the aims of the activities we devised and informing her of the progress she was making. For developing the fine motor skills she needed, we encouraged scribbling, and the attempts to draw which followed from this. We tried for large free arm movements through chalking on the big blackboard and gave patient instruction in the art of holding scissors so that they will cut. Again, this was, besides a straightforward educational aim, intended to have a pervasive beneficial effect on Evelyn's self-concept. Children who, like Evelyn, know they are likely to fail, often do so out of the sheer muscular tension resulting from the intensity of the effort with which they attempt to muster their forces. Relaxation is then most easily taught as the opposite sensation to tension, so alternate deliberate hand stiffening, followed by shaking the hand loosely from the wrist, is one of the variety of experiences through which the child can learn to recognize for himself when he is in a fit state to begin to draw or write. The kind of clumsiness which Evelyn showed is also frequently met in children who have learning or language problems; in itself it tells the teacher little, since it may arise from a variety of antecedent causes. Anxiety has already been mentioned. Poor motor organization as a cause may or may not be linked with damage to the central nervous system. Common sense suggests we should enquire if the child has had a growing spell recently; he may not have adjusted his reaching techniques to suit the extra length of his arms. Similarly a recent illness from which the child has not yet fully recovered may be to blame.

Evelyn's language programme was thus very broadly based. And as relationships were established and her confidence built up, we saw the new Evelyn emerge: a determined, curious, happy and very likeable little girl, whose muttered words had become language. On one occasion, when I asked her if she had been for a ride in a car, her answer expanded to: 'No, my dad 'aven't took me in a car.' Her misuse of rules was probably more the effect of local dialect than the over-generalization of rules occurring at about three-years-old. Over-generalized use of rules and babyish articulation should in any case not by themselves be considered as sufficient evidence of language delay; children who begin to talk earlier than the norm may acquire these traits as habits, not easily lost. At six plus, with increased interaction with other schoolchildren these pseudo speech defects usually drop out (see Gulliford, 1971 Ch 6).

Evelyn's determination, at six, to learn to copy her name, showed she was able to use language as mediator of a task in a way which overcame one of her disabilities. She had learned the meaning of direction: up, down and sideways were no longer mysteries. She could hold a pencil effectively. But visuo-motor difficulties were defeating all efforts to make the pencil go in the direction she intended. After much preliminary practice, when surprising but unwanted results were obtained, Evelyn and I were both becoming frustrated by the gap between her competence and her performance. I proposed that, instead of my continuing to tell her which way to go, she should herself tell her hand to go sideways. Evelyn bent a frowning look on the offending hand, and fairly bawled at it: 'Hand, go sideways.' Her hand shot sideways, the mark was made, and we had a procedure established for future use. Her pride in the achievement of the copied letters was immense.

But the greater revelation of functional changes in Evelyn came soon after this, during her play with a kaleidoscope which has alternative top-pieces which can, with some difficulty, be fitted into it. Evelyn picked up the spare piece, announcing: 'I like this other one best.' I replied that I would have to change it over for her as it was so awkward: and did so. She gave it a cursory look, then, 'I want the other one on now.' In a sort of mock horror, I exclaimed, 'What, already?' She grinned, replying, 'I might be able to get this one on.'

Now it is by no means the mere difficulty of this structurally complex reply, nor even her newfound confidence in her ability to do something judged difficult, which is impressive here. For Evelyn, in replying not just to what I had said, but to its underlying meaning, showed skill in that type of social interaction which is needed to make our responses appropriate.

The absorption of knowledge of rules or norms, makes this possible. Cicourel (1973), following the ideas of Schutz on this topic, generalizes it like this:

The question-answer sequencing requires a reciprocal rule whereby my question provides a basis (reason) for your answer while the possibility of a future question from you provides a basis (reason) for my question. When I ask a question I have intentions (a deep structure) or a more elaborated version in mind than what I actually ask you. My 'pruned' or 'deleted' surface question, therefore, presumes a more elaborated version which I assume you 'fill in', despite receiving only my surface message. Your answer, therefore, is based upon both the elaborated and surface elements of my question, and I in turn 'fill in' your answer so as to construct your elaborated intentions. Both participants, therefore, must presume that each will generate recognizable and intelligible utterances as a necessary condition for the interaction to even occur, and each must reconstruct the other's intentions (the deep structure) if there is to be co-ordinated social interaction. (p 34)

To see what really happened in the interchange between Evelyn and myself, we have to expand it to make explicit the hidden elements recognized by us as participants. To do this, we have to take into account the situation in which it occurred, non-verbal signs (facial expressions) intonation and word stress (which can alter meanings considerably), the meanings behind the words used, and the way the replies are framed on the basis of earlier conversations.

First, the situation. I was circulating among the children, talking with each in turn, thus indicating that they were free to go on with their self-chosen activity. Had I been teaching a specific skill, I would have called one child to work with me at my desk. So Evelyn knew she had choice in what she did, and that she was to direct her own activity.

What I then conveyed with my 'What, already?' spoken with some emphasis, and, no doubt, raised eyebrows plus head and eye movements, went something like this:

You've already had it changed to the one you said you wanted yet you haven't bothered to look at that properly: so tell me, why do you want it changed again, when I should be moving on and giving my attention to someone else?

Evelyn's quick grin showed recognition of the un-serious teasing element in my deliberate exaggeration. Her own reply, 'I might be able to get this one on,' was framed so that it made creative use of the type of language ideas she had gleaned from many previous conversations. It could be expanded something like this:

Yes, I know all about that, but what I really wanted was to change it myself, and since you're the one who's always telling me I can learn to do things for myself if I keep trying, I don't see what you're grumbling about, and anyway, I know you don't really mind if I change my mind about what I want.

On this basis of unspoken understanding, I could watch Evelyn struggle until she had successfully effected the changeover. Our reciprocal interaction had led to changes in behaviour. For Evelyn these could be far-reaching. The effects of social learning through successful imitation (using rules won from observation of adults) are considered by Danziger (1971) to involve changes in the learner's self-concept, while reinforcement by impersonal external rewards does not. He writes:

In social learning it is not only the source of the reward which is personal, but the outcome has a personal significance too. The learner has become a different person by acquiring some of the actions of another person. (p 69)

Now this change in self-concept through the extension of role repertoire is of great importance to 'normal' children. I suggest that it is crucial for children whose disabilities or social position have resulted in many failure experiences, who thus have notions about their own likely performance which are both realistically low and unrealistically and unnecessarily low. Evelyn's success in manipulating the situation through language use, as well as her success in her self-chosen task, indicate to the teacher that the 'turn' has been made; Evelyn has acquired techniques for dealing with her extra learning difficulties as a minimally but multiply-handicapped child, which had been concealing her normal ability to assimilate experience in the form of interactional procedures.

This everyday practical reasoning is embedded in all our thinking activities, whether it be in the coding and 'chunking' of information for remembering, or in the formulating of abstract rules to perceive relationships. Precisely because it is embedded, it may go unacknowledged.

The schemes of reference we hold in common are used

automatically, therefore we are unaware of them. We do it without thinking, so we do not stop to think of the predicament of someone who for some reason has not internalized this kind of interpretative procedure. This is a problem for the handicapped child where the normal socialization processes of early childhood have been interrupted or are incomplete; a situation particularly likely to affect the late talker. This leads me to my second example of the needs of a child with language disability.

Susan is now 14 years old, assessed as ESN (S) some years previously. She has an unusually shaped palate which makes her speech difficult to understand if you don't know her. Her sensitivity about her poor articulation leads her to avoid or restrict conversations. I had come to know her when she was 13, as she was one of several ESN (S) children who took part in the testing of my experimental language programme (which follows from Graham's work) based on increasing structural difficulty of sentences rather than on vocabulary or length of sentence, which I hoped would help in narrowing the gap between these children's competence and their language performance (Meers, 1972). While Susan's expressive language was far below the norm for her age, the success which she gained in demonstrating comprehension of the material presented, her enjoyment of the tasks and the fact that she realized that I understood what she did say, led her to talk freely to me from that time. We have since had a number of conversations while I have been on playground duty, which have dealt with some problem which was worrying her. I select one.

Susan: 'Do you know why I don't like coming to school?' I encouraged her to tell me. She replied: 'It's because everyone keeps telling me what a big girl I'm getting.'

I thought about this, recalling that she had a horror, normal to her age, of being thought fat; and that she might have only a limited concept of 'big', equating it in meaning with 'fat'. I explained the remark to Susan, showing how it was used as praise for her sensible attitudes. Her face cleared. 'Oh, I didn't know what it meant.' Not knowing what it means, having to puzzle out not only words but facial expression, gestures, social situations, do without factual knowledge which we assume in ordinary situations, can impede mental functioning through distracting attention, causing confusion and misunderstanding, preventing remembering. The provision of many explanations, the building up of broad concepts rich with many meanings, is also a responsibility of the teacher of language disabled children.

My third example concerns Leroy, aged seven, whose problems seem to fall mainly into the category of children whose language disturbance is closely linked with more general disturbance, which appears to rest on deprivation or separation experiences at an early age. His pattern of bizarre and obsessive actions is met with in children who have either been child-minded in the worst of circumstances or who have been left safely locked in a room while mother went to work. As Leroy gradually came to interact, at times, with other children, sometimes playing football with the younger ones, a moment arose when it seemed I might get a reply if I spoke to him. Asking 'What colour's your ball, Leroy?' I expected the answer 'Blue', but Leroy said, 'It's a blue one.'

This correct, over-precise type of answer supports by its rigidity the view that the infrequency of Leroy's spontaneous speech results less from inability than unwillingness to commit himself to the possible dangers of too much interaction. Again, an oddity in his style appeared when, after initial resistance, he took notice of what I was telling him about why he could not play in a certain place, at that time. 'Ah, miss, look, the ceiling is breaking itself.' Personalization of dolls and toys is common enough, but the personalization of a ceiling was new to me, and again indicative of a difference in interpretative procedures between us. Such slight but pertinent fragments have to be noted and assessed together with more conventional clues.

Whether the usual programme of stimulation is judged enough to bring results, or whether it is supplemented by methods such as those I have described, which aim to improve underlying functions, the interacting adult is the key to progress. Nothing could be more discouraging to the teacher than to receive no verbal response to what is said, but we have to be knowledgeable enough, persistent enough, and hopeful enough, to continue to feed in language experience in relevant situations. In time, a response will come. This will in its turn develop new forms of attention, imagining, feeling, and thinking in the child (Gulliford, 1960). Thus, the prime need is to improve the ratio of well-informed adults to children in our Special schools, if we wish to intervene decisively to improve the children's level of functioning.

From this it will be seen that I believe as good a theory as we can work out about what language is and does, should underlie and inform our teaching. My overall emphasis, as a teacher speaking to teachers, is on how to teach better from gaining better insight into the learning – teaching process. For language is more than a tool for thinking, or means of communication or a standardized form. We use it for so many things that, paradoxically, it cannot be used to fully describe itself.

In the following chapters, I try to indicate some of the thinking behind my suggestions for helping the non-talker; the rationale which is needed for the teacher's work to remain individualized and inventive.

2

How do we learn language?

Even the poorest, most limited use of language is qualitatively different from the calls and emotive sounds used by animals, for there are significant differences between human language and the communicative systems of animals and insects. Hockett (1960) describes these and Menyuk (1971) discusses them. I want to single out four essential differences, which Hockett calls displacement, productivity, duality of patterning and transmission.

Displacement refers to the ability of the human speaker to talk about events or objects which are remote from the speakers, either in time or place, or both. This is another way of pointing out that we use symbolism. A satirical description of what would happen if we tried to dispense with this abstract method occurs in *Gulliver's Travels*. Swift describes 'a scheme for entirely abolishing all words whatsoever'. The proposal was, that for 'convenience, health and brevity', all participants in potential conversations should carry about with them 'such things as were necessary to express the particular business they are to discourse on'. Then Swift has Gulliver comment on the result of this scheme for expression by use of things:

I have often beheld two of these sages almost sinking under the weight of their packs, like pedlars amongst us, who when they meet in the streets would lay down their loads, open their sacks and hold conversation for an hour together, then put up their implements, help each other resume their burthens, and take their leave.

Even so, these 'sages' would clearly have difficulty in referring to absent, past, or future events, and the problems of representing complex ideas would be even greater. And the possibility of success would depend on the people concerned having a prior knowledge, and a shared knowledge, of the language system and of the general body of ideas current in the society they lived in. The idea of 'displacement' involves previously acquired concepts.

Productivity refers to our ability to combine, and recombine, elements from this symbolic system, in new ways. It refers to the creative aspect of our language use, its quality of unlimited expansion into new meanings, new combinations of thoughts, feelings, ideas. Although animals have a repertoire of emotional and social signals — warning, notification of food, territorial boundaries — these only permit small variations. Not only can they not be rearranged to form new vocalizations, they have to be triggered off by a situation; their use is largely involuntary. The 'openness' of 'productivity' implies that we have a choice. The move away from the arbitrary is linked with the need for language not to be a random collection of elements. For an illustration of this, I again turn to Swift's satire. He describes another 'project', a contrivance which is said to enable people to write books without the trouble either of acquiring knowledge or taking thought, in the following manner.

Thirty-six boys, for six hours a day, turned a handle on a machine which changed the order of words which were pasted on it at random. The new arrangement of words was then read out and any chance fragments of sentences recorded. From piecing together this collection, and scraps from five hundred more such collections, the professor hoped to give the world 'a complete body of all arts and sciences'.

Swift's satire points out to us the absurdity of considering language as a mere collection of parts of speech, plus a large vocabulary, put together by chance. Its potentiality requires a system.

Duality of patterning refers to the economical use we can make of the limited number of sounds which we can discriminate. By arranging and re-arranging these sounds, we can extend our vocabulary to fulfil our needs.

Language transmits information across generations and cultures to a far greater extent than animal communication ever can. Although bird calls are learned by imitation from the parent, and higher animals teach their young the skills involved in food-getting and self-protection, much of the animal's learned lore dies with him. Language, spoken and especially written, enables knowledge to become cumulative and readily available. The individual child does not have to recreate all that has been previously learned; he inherits the culture which rests on what other people have found out before him.

Hockett's criteria of difference can thus be expressed in parallel terms; displacement is made possible by symbolism; productivity by structure, or combinatory rules. Duality of patterning enables us to use a large number of words. This has a two-fold effect. On the one hand, the fact that we can extend vocabulary means that we can define and refine experience, express subtleties and shades of meaning. On the other hand, it is linked with the ability to express meaning through different forms of symbolic communication. Examples are the patterning used in Morse Code, where long and short pulses are combined to convey varied complex messages;

finger spelling with deaf people, Braille with blind, the language of the drums to send distant messages in Africa, musical notation, mathematical systems, and their representation through the symbol of a symbol.

Transmission can be seen as a cultural tool which extends the possibilities open to the individual member of society. In pre-literate societies, the bards developed complex systems for remembering the myth, history, lore and legend which explained, entertained and taught the members of that particular culture. Surviving examples which were written down as the society became literate, such as the *Odyssey*, more or less in the form that the story was told, have overpassed the boundary of time and culture. Industrial technology is a recent development in man's history. With the vastly increased amount of sheer information which it needs if it is to thrive, it demanded literacy, the written word which could reach so many more people so much more quickly than by word of mouth. Yet it is only a form of language use, dependent on the basic ability to listen, to understand and to use inner language, as well as to speak; and it is supplemented by information from such forms as broadcasting and television.

There are alternative ways of looking at differences between human and animal communication. One is to regard the development of language as *continuous* from animal behaviour, the other as *discontinuous*. The distinction is of considerable importance for theories of how language works, and therefore of how we can best teach it.

The continuity theory states that the roots of language may be found in animal communication, with the differences between the two forms seen as resulting from man's increase in general intelligence. This supposes that it is possible to compare as on an absolute scale, the very different kinds of ability which occur in different species. Lenneberg (1967) warns that behaviour should always be considered as it applies to a particular species. This criticism of the continuity idea also applies to the problem of comparison between the ways some animals learn in certain laboratory situations, and the ways that people learn in everyday situations. The behaviourist school, which relies on the notion of conditioning by experience, sees learning as stimulus followed by response. Language acquisition is explained along similar lines. Skinner, in *Verbal Behaviour* (1957), considers language as a series of verbal responses which in some way generalize from combinations already experienced. This theory seemed not to account for many features of language. Attempts to overcome the difficulty of lack of meaning led Osgood and others to propose mediating processes between the stimulus and the response. The language model which resulted from this considers language as a number of separate sub-skills arising on independent bases, but each affecting the working of the whole system. A well known expression of this is the Illinois Test of Psycholinguistic Abilities (I.T.P.A.), which lists skills which are said, though with little supporting evidence, to work together to produce language ability.

The symbolic mediating processes between the stimulus and the response cannot by their nature be observed, but they are said to put in meaningfulness to the process of response to words, which in turn stimulates appropriate responses to these words. As in information theory, also current in the fifties when the model was worked out, it assumes that it is the probability, based on previous conditioning, that a certain response will occur, that causes it to do so.

A contrasting and fundamentally different model of what language involves was first proposed by Chomsky in 1957. This new psycholinguistic theory sought to analyze language 'rules'. These are postulated to account for the ability of human beings to speak and understand words which are arranged in sentences new to the speaker of them and the listener to them. Our unconscious knowledge of the underlying abstract rules of language, its 'deep' structure, is known as 'competence'. When words are formulated into spoken language, the sounds, the meanings and the 'surface' grammatical arrangements make up the 'performance' aspect of language.

Chomsky argues (1967, 1968) that although different world languages have many superficial differences, such as whether word order affects meaning, their underlying rule structures have common features, 'universals', which express man's unique attributes, his particular ways of thinking, rather than his greater 'intelligence'. Chomsky is thus very strongly for discontinuity with animal calls or gestures, and devotes some space to pointing out the differences. He considers (1968) that it may be an example of 'emergence', that is 'the appearance of a qualitatively different [*biological*] phenomenon at a specific stage of complexity of organism.' (p 329)

One of the difficulties in understanding what Chomsky is really getting at lies in the strangeness to non-linguists of some of the terminology used, and also, perhaps, the memory of 'grammar' lessons at school which have convinced many only that they are non-competent in this area. So it may be reassuring to state that the more technical aspects of the theoretical constructs developed by Chomsky between 1957 and 1965 are less important for the teacher than an understanding that language ability is splendidly creative. It is this creative aspect which is highlighted in the now famous sentence: 'Colourless green ideas sleep furiously.' We can all produce and understand things which are unlikely to have heard before; what we know about the grammar, meaning and sound aspects of our native language helps us to recognize and categorize regardless of how often we hear words, or our previous conditioning. The very fixedness of the underlying laws, which can generate anything that can be said through recombining and reordering form and meaning, give to the individual language user his infinite scope for invention. This is generative transformational grammar: control of rules brings freedom to create. This means that we all have a capacity, which needs to be set off by appropriate stimulation, for language. It does not mean that there are no individual differences in its use, but these are seen as less important than the similarities. Chomsky (1968) writes:

As participants in a certain culture we are naturally aware of the great differences in ability to use language, in knowledge of vocabulary, and so on, that result from differences in native ability and from differences in conditions of our acquisition; we naturally pay much less attention to the similarities and to common knowledge, which we take for granted. But if we manage to establish the requisite psychic distance, if we actually compare the generative grammar that must be postulated for different speakers of the same language, we find that the similarities that we take for granted are quite marked and that the divergencies are few and marginal. What is more, it seems that dialects that are superficially quite remote, even barely intelligible on first contact, share a vast central core of common rules and processes and differ very slightly in underlying structure, which seem to remain invariant through long historical eras. (p 339)

The 'underlying structures', or 'core of common rules and processes' which Chomsky refers to, are linked by him to the notion of an 'innate structure' of mind which, he suggests, would make it possible for each child to acquire language. This would be done by the child comparing the language samples that he hears from adults with his skeleton rule system, to find out which particular one of the potential languages it belongs to. In this way, says Chomsky, he can extend his knowledge beyond his experience and decide how much of what he hears is a defective or deviant sample.

That is the 'strong' form of the theory that people have a special pre-disposition towards language. The 'weak' form of this theory points to certain ways of organizing experience through conceptual thinking, through selection and reduction of stimuli to a form which is condensed enough to be processed and stored in memory, a set of pre-dispositions, the ability to form integrated patterns of perception, as it were, which are set in motion by the social context of the family: what Lenneberg calls the 'resonance' effect.

Braine (1971) has discussed aspects of Chomsky's theory, considering that it is most fruitful to think about Chomsky's proposal that learning proceeds by comparing heard sentences with 'hypothetical' grammar systems, whether these are regarded as innate or not. Braine points out how difficult Chomsky's test procedure would be to operate. Not only do the sentences the child hears have to be clearly identifiable, that is, correct examples; there also has to be some information about what are negative instances, not allowed by the grammar of his language. This does not mean just an incomplete or bungled sentence, such as occurs naturally in speech. We are able to ignore a mistake because there are usually so many other clues, so much 'redundancy' in spoken language. The examples Braine gives are that while we can say either 'Help George do it', or 'Help George to do it', we can only say 'Allow George to do it', and 'Let George do it'. Non-sentences such as 'Allow George do it' and 'Let George to do it', would not be told to the child as what not to say; nor is there anything to show that he could make use of such information even if he had it.

This argument leads Braine to suggest a process whereby the acquisition of grammar could be considered as the perceptual learning of patterns. In his model, two components are needed. First there is the 'scanner', which, as it receives the heard sentences, or 'input', observes its properties of patterning, and registers these in a kind of intermediate memory store. Once the initial input has been thus registered, there is something against which new inputs can be compared, and new, differing instances recorded in their turn. When an input is recognized as having the same pattern as a previously registered example, it is moved on to the next intermediate memory store. Eventually constantly recurring instances will be moved on into the permanent memory store. Thus the second component required in this model would be an ordered series of memory stores, its final level containing the learned rules or 'pattern properties' of the language.

The purpose of the intermediate levels would be in the losing, or forgetting, of wrong or random examples, which do not move on through the recording system simply because they are dissimilar to each other. A second proposed advantage would be that abstract properties rather than specific ones would be readily learned. As Braine puts it:

This tendency follows from the fact that the properties learned fastest are those that are shared by many sentences and thus recur frequently. In general, the intermediate stores act as a kind of sieve which retains what is systematic in the input. Specific properties will be subject to repeated forgetting and restorage, although those that recur often enough will of course be learned — among them the exceptions and special cases which are so common in natural languages. (p 79)

The 'scanner' would not only be in touch with information in the form of incoming sentences but would also incorporate a 'recognition routine', through the access it would have to the permanent memory store. Information already learned could then be used for more complex grouping, and for listing specific properties.

This ingenious system would require a highly complex and sensitive scanning mechanism. Like the Chomsky model, it postulates language universals; unlike the Chomsky model of innate ability, it suggests the scanner is 'present' to notice and pick up the essentials. It would need to possess an innate, unlearned system of priorities, that is a set of discovery procedures for grammar acquisition, which is said to allow for learning to proceed from general to specific properties, without needing to have statements about what is not grammatical. Braine also describes a generally similar proposal by Kelly in which learning takes place through confirmation by repetition, and unlearning by forgetting.

A very different criticism of Chomsky is made by Campbell and Wales (1970). Their point is that Chomsky's term 'competence', the unhampered ability within, is not sufficiently worked out. Because Chomsky and other linguists try and study what language is rather than what it is in use, Campbell and Wales say that 'competence' has been too restricted, omitting what seems to them to be a most important component of linguistic ability. They refer to the appropriateness of the utterance in its situation and verbal context. They therefore argue that an adequate psychology of language has to take into account the context it is used in, as well as being able to explain how it can be creative, how it can generate new forms. They name this 'communicative competence', seeing it as resting on interactions between predisposition and environment. They suggest ways of trying to explain how this 'communicative competence' can be acquired, without reaching firm conclusions. One suggestion is that the child's question or demand, parental response, and the child's response to this, might be a fruitful field of study in clarifying what happens when the child begins to talk.

Piaget (1971) has proposed that there are grounds for 'suspending Chomsky's innatism while preserving the rest of his theory' (p 90). He proposes that the problem of whether language acquisition should be considered as an innate genetically programmed scheme, or an acquisition from experience, could be solved by a third possibility; the process of 'internal equilibriation'. By this he means the abilities, knowledge, patterns of expectancy and so forth, which the child develops in the sensori-motor period of development from birth to two years. So this development period would supply the basis. Instead of everything being contained in advance, 'layer by layer *construction* would have to take the place of *axiomatization*' (p 9).

This would allow for the expansion of the theory of what language is, taking into account some of the features that even transformational grammar cannot explain, through the notion of 'transformational fields', or 'linguistic structures' such as Piaget refers to as being developed by Saumjan.

As Piaget points out:

. . . the relatively late appearance of language in the course of the second year of life seems to confirm the constructionist thesis. For why should speech begin at this level of development and not earlier? Contrary to the too facile explanations by conditioning, which imply that language acquisition starts as early as the second month, the acquisition of language presupposes the prior formation of sensori-motor intelligence, which goes to justify Chomsky's ideas concerning the necessity of a prelinguistic substrata akin to rationality. But this intelligence, which antedates speech, is very far from preformed from the beginning; we can see it grow step by step out of the gradual co-ordination of assimilation schemes. (p 91)

For Piaget, language is a limited (though very important) segment of the symbolic function, which includes, besides language, all forms of imitation, representional play, imagery, which are considered along with the development of representation and thought. This explains why deaf-mute children also play make-believe games and develop a language of gestures. There are grounds for considering that these alternative symbolic systems are not only parallel with language in developing, but may also be prior to it. Cicourel (1973) discusses this in the context of 'assumed social meanings' which we unconsciously use in interpreting what people say:

The discussion of interpretative features can help us understand the speaker-hearer's production and comprehension of non-oral communication and, in particular, the manual signing and finger-spelling of the deaf. The hearing child's acquisition of non-oral features of communication is viewed as natural and integral to his acquisition of oral speech, suggesting that such features are as basic as, if not prior to, the child's facility with oral communication. The generative nature of sign language usage for the deaf and the use of non-oral features of communication among hearing persons are not viewed as being tied to a syntactic rule production system, but as having features that mark sign language as a qualitatively distinct system for the deaf, and as a residual system for the hearing that either adds supplementary information to oral speech or can transcend such speech and serve as an independent channel of communication. I am assuming that the hearing child first learns a rather primitive signal system consisting of gestures, quasi-manual signs and vocal cues. As his speech production grows more sophisticated, the use of the signal system becomes residual and subject to minimal control. If speech is not encouraged or is blocked, the manual sign system would emerge as the basic form of communication. I am asserting that the generative semantic principles underlying both hearing and deaf systems of communication are the same. (p 94–5)

What is interesting here is Cicourel's reference to processes such as gestures, which become residual when more sophisticated processes such as speech take over the main function. There seems to have been little investigation into the role and importance of primitive systems which lend support in childhood and later tend to drop out, although Sapir does refer to auditory and motor imagery, as the 'historic' fountainhead of speech and thinking. Eidetic imagery (or 'photographic memory'), commonly met with in children, but rare in adults, receives little attention; yet, as Piaget points out, the role of imagery in the sensori-motor period of the child's development may well be a main bridge between motor actions, perceptions, and the development of thought. He refers to the role of the image in prolonging experience as 'an indispensable auxiliary in the functioning of the very dynamism of thought'. By prolonging the image it enables it to be processed, internalized and stored with other like experiences.

The stages by which this happens may be summarized: imitation by the child, which becomes representation, as when he pretends to be asleep: then deferred imitation, such as in putting a doll to sleep. What has previously happened to the child has been remembered or become internalized in the form of images. These can then be used by the child to anticipate further acts. Language is seen by Piaget as having the same roots (and, in the beginning, the same function) as symbolic play, deferred imitation, mental images and affective development. The differences between symbolic play and language lie in the fact that play requires an object which has some link with the object or event it is to represent. For instance, a child may use a brick to represent a train, or any other object to stand for what he wants to manipulate in play, but he does use some actual thing. Language dispenses with this physical link. The symbols of language are arbitrary and conventionally accepted within a whole culture, while play symbols are usually personal. Play consists either of isolated incidents or loosely linked episodes, whereas words, as we have seen, are formed into much tighter systems.

The importance for educationists of the 'experience', 'innate', 'equilibration' tags lies in the kind of teaching – learning situations which we organize for children. The mother-child relationship provides one such form of learning situation, from which teachers may be able to learn how the interaction between mother and child affects the way the mother talks to, imitates and replies to her child. She will tend to speak more simply, more slowly, more clearly and in complete short sentences rather than in our usual unclear, incomplete or plain ungrammatical normal spoken usage. This happens without the mother making a conscious effort and without her receiving specific training in how to do this. It is an example of interactional procedures by which we unnoticingly regulate many other features of our life. That it is so is shown by the frequency with which, as the child acquires expressive speech, families come to adopt their children's private names for family pets, etc., or pick up the defective pronunciation of their child, as with the professor who gravely enquired of his tea-time guest, 'Would you care for a choccy bic-bic ?'

Nelson (1973) describes from a detailed one-year study of 18 children of middle-class white American parents, the different strategies which children and their parents use. The children were 10 to 15 months old when the study began, so it was concerned with the children's first words, and short sentences as they started to come in.

One of the difficulties in describing early child language is the way one talks about their first words, which clearly are not just single words in the adult sense. Because they appear to mean the same thing as a whole sentence of adult talk they are often called 'holophrases' i.e., one word used as a sentence. Nelson points out that the 'holophrase' notion is acceptable as an idea that the child's first words carry relational meaning, but that children's thought is not really describable in the same terms as adult thought.

Analyzing the words the children did use showed that two types of language use could be discerned. Some of the children learned first to talk about things (object language), but others preferred words about themselves and other people (social interaction language). Only the first ten words entering into the children's spoken vocabulary showed much measure of agreement: these included Mommy (15 of the 18), Daddy (13), dog (11), hi (10), ball (8). The differences then increased considerably, but there were a high number of animal names, mostly referring not to their own pets, but to toys, neighbourhood pets, pictures. Food items, as might be expected, were the next most numerous category, with toys, vehicles, household items, also represented. Nelson's discussion on the children's criteria for selecting words is enlightening in the way it relates language acquisition to the child's method of actively structuring his world:

Frequency of personal experience, exposure to words, strength of need or desire cannot apparently explain the selection of these words. They are personal, selective, and for the most part action related. It is apparent that children learn the names of things they can act on, whether they are toys, shoes, scissors, money, keys, blankets, or bottles as well as things that act themselves such as dogs and cars. They do not learn the names of things in the house or outside that are simply 'there' whether these are tables, plates, towels, grass, or stores . . . The common attribute of all the most frequent early referents is that they have salient properties of change – that is, they do things (roll, run, bark, meow, go rrr, and drive away). In this connection, sound is as relevant as movement; both exhibit temporal change. The omissions are in general of things that – however obvious and important – just sit there: sofas, tables, chest, windows, plates, overalls, trees, grass. The words that are learned are not only the ones the child acts upon in some way (shoes, bottle, ball), but also ones that do something themselves, that the child only observes – trucks, clocks, buses and all the animals. (Although some animal names referred to pictures rather than live or toy animals, the mother almost always gave the animal sound: e.g. 'What does the tiger say? r-r-r'. The sound rather than the picture thus may define the concept.) This general conclusion is of course in accord with cognitive theories (e.g. Piaget's) emphasizing the importance of the child's action to his definition of the world, but it implicates equally the importance of actions external to the child. Thus, the words the child learns reflect the child's mode of structuring the world. (pp 31, 33)

Nelson's findings about the relationships between the type of words first used, comprehension ability, the type of maternal response, and the rate at which language developed are also interesting. She found that the children who first referred to things rather than using 'expressive' or social language progressed more rapidly. One might speculate here that this could be an effect of the type of personality which is highly regarded in a given society, and the way traits conducive to developing 'outgoing' rather than 'introverted' personalities are reinforced by social approval.

Early interest in language and comprehension of it, and use of standard phrases, were shown to be good indicators of rapid progress. The children who showed comprehension did not all talk as much in the early days of the study. Some who talked more might have been 'testing' to see whether their speech was acceptable. Other children may have less need of verification because they rely more on their own internal processing of the language they hear. All the mothers used complete sentences three or four words long when talking to their children; tests showed that this type of sentence was responded to by the children better than one-word or incomplete utterances.

The amount that the child talked in a play situation was also positively related to rapid development in the second year. Spontaneous imitation of spoken words was shown to be more useful to the child before the age of two than after that age. More questions were asked at two by more advanced speakers. Accuracy of articulation at two was not related either to earlier or later performance. Where the mother responded to the child's behaviour, his language accelerated although, as we have seen, where the mother directed the child's behaviour it grew more slowly.

Nelson proposes that the young child's way of learning to speak involves a concept-matching model. The child's concepts of objects, events and relationships may overlap with those referred to by adult language. The correct or incorrect notions of the child determine how the word is applied by him, and whether he continues to try and apply the word to that concept. Individual differences in modes of tackling the problem of what to make of the world are involved here, since it suggests that children will attend to different features of the environment.

The primitive rule system of the young child, as well as the slow process of freeing the word from the object it refers to, provide ample evidence for the long slow growth of language ability. As rules begin to be acquired and overgeneralized by their use in situations analagous to their correct use, the child's ways of thinking are demonstrated. For instance, the three-year-old who, in reply to his questions 'Is that . . .?' had been told 'Well actually it's . . .', greeted the sight of the first real cricket match he went to, (as opposed to the Test Match on T.V.) with 'Oh look, actual cricket.' He is using analogy to get the word 'actual'.

At this three-year-old stage, the child is sufficiently sure of his basic family relationships to branch out into a wider social sphere. Playing with (or perhaps alongside) friends becomes important to him. This provides an added source of language learning opportunity. In the interchange between children, the effort to express oneself in a way which is understood by the other, pushes the child on to develop standardized grammar, vocabulary and pronunciation. The marked difference between three and four-year-olds with the increase in genuinely cooperative play and other social skills occurring around this age, has been linked with Brannon's (1968) findings that the four-year-olds used significantly more 'transformations' (their sentences were more complex) as well as expanded their sentences much more than three-year-olds. I suggest the importance of the nursery school teacher in creating situations where these interchanges may take place between children, and, herself, providing a sufficiently large and interesting stock of language examples to the child. This can be partly through her own spoken language with the children, and with other adults; and also by adding different types of repertoire through the language of nursery rhymes, poems, told stories, and stories read from books, which are vitally necessary, since the child needs to know what language sounds like when it is written down. Unless he is sufficiently familiar with this aspect of language he is unlikely to achieve fluency when he is at the reading stage of language use. Thus knowledge of well-formed and varied sentence forms comes from what is heard. A large and flexible vocabulary comes mainly from experience which provides the concepts which fill words with meanings. 'Nouns' come from observing and asking, 'verbs' from doing things.

The term used by Campbell and Wales (1970), 'communicative competence', seems needed to describe what a child has to learn about language to make the response which is novel but appropriate. The amount of mental organization needed for it, which has been developing from the child's earliest weeks of life, suggests that much more goes on in the earlier development stages than Chomsky allows for.

But the enormous amount of work, both faithfully acclaiming and fiercely critical, that has stemmed from Chomsky's work and spilled over into psychology and sociology, is its own tribute to the scope and boldness of the Chomskyan approach. In this respect he is a parallel figure to Piaget. It may be through the meeting and marrying of their approaches that further insights have come which radically alter the way problems of how people learn are now looked at by psychologists. Together with this goes the problem of what makes people want to learn.

More than ever the importance of arousal, surprise, curiosity, attention; its maintenance through contrast and variety, reinforcement through the very pleasure of the dynamic event of enlarging experience, knowing the purpose and direction of one's activity, are considered as motivating agents. No one optimum method of presentation of material or unique sequence of learning steps can be postulated in this relativistic view of how people learn. But it does involve applying certain principles, such as Bruner (1966) enumerates; predispositions, forms of presentation, sequences of presentation, reinforcements, and how these can be marshalled in the effort to assist and shape growth; to enable the process of knowing, that is, thinking for oneself, to become operative. It is to what happens, from the baby stage to the development of mature language ability, that we turn in the next chapter.

3
What happens as the child learns language

The first sound made by a baby is, as every mother knows, the cry. Soon this is differentiated into several types of crying sound, supplemented by a range of vowel sounds. These have been grouped by Lewis (1963) into 'discomfort' and 'comfort' sounds.

As well as making sounds himself, the baby is developing his abilities to respond to sound. He learns to attend and so to listen, then to discover what events are linked with things he hears, sees, or touches. His learning of what to expect from life is thus beginning in these early weeks. There is some evidence, though as yet it is slender, that these abilities may be present very early in life.

We can see how rapidly progress is taking place. At one month the child shows 'startle' on hearing sounds. This is an involuntary response, a 'reflex' movement. He also appears to discriminate his mother's voice, and to prefer it to other people's (Mills and Melhuish, 1974). By three months a definite eye movement, by which he tries to investigate sounds he hears, shows he can tell where the sound comes from. At four or five months, when he can support his head reasonably well, he turns it towards the source of the sound. But when the sound is presented more than a few times, he loses interest. His response stops. Already he is a creature who rouses to the unexpected, who seeks the novel event.

Vocally, this is expressed in the coos and chuckles with which he greets people and new sights and sounds, recognizes familiar settings. When he cries with hunger, he may stop when he hears his mother's approaching footsteps. So recognition has advanced to anticipation of a regularly occurring event.

Physically, he shows bodily activity through which he seeks to investigate, as in looking at, reaching for, and grasping at toys. This is an important developmental step. The analysis by Woodward (1971) of the series of coordinated responses required for picking up a rattle and shaking it, shows it to be a sequence of five actions: moving the hand towards the rattle, opening the hand, closing it round the rattle, lifting and shaking it. This kind of experienced activity leads on to the planning of behaviour, and later on to the extraction of rules which are useful for efficient problem solving. The early development of such abilities as reaching and grasping is not only important for skills such as these; it is also important for the development of visual perception itself. While the ability to see, as well as to hear, seems to be present soon after birth, it is in active exploration that the child alters his perceptual experience, learning to interpret such features of the world as the size, shape and distance of objects (Haber and Hershenson, 1973).

White (1971) has shown how this sort of reaching and grasping achievement can be brought forward in time by the provision of suitable visual stimulation. Even putting red and white striped mittens on the babies' hands resulted in lowering the average age at which they moved their fists into their range of vision and studied them.

I am adopting the position that our experiences lead to complex interlocked sequences of actions and perceptions. Even an apparently simple 'automatic' movement pattern, such as the synchronization of head and eye movements in turning to look at and follow a moving target with the eye, turns out to involve such a sequence of integrated moves. Bizzi (1974) has shown with monkeys and with men that when an object comes unexpectedly into the field of vision, an orderly sequence of movements is set in train. First a fast eye movement takes the fovea, the most sensitive and visually acute part of the retina, to its desired target. Then, after a brief delay, the head turns in the same direction. The eyes then have to rotate back again to compensate for the overshoot. To achieve the fixation of the target, a number of computations have had to be made, including the angular distance between the initial lines of sight and the position of the target. Bizzi found that what was observed to happen could be explained along the following lines. A centrally initiated movement of eye and head is modified by receptors within the ear which are activated by the head turning. These receptors are responsible for the compensatory eye movements which keep the eye on its target. So the programme begun in the central nervous system is modified by feedback from information coming to the brain from sensory systems in the body. In this way errors can be corrected, the two sources of information interacting to produce a smooth performance.

When the animal or person is able to anticipate the appearance of the object, the sequence is altered. In this predictive mode, the head turning begins before the eye moves, and different muscular combinations are involved. How the switch from one mode to the other is made, remains mysterious. Even more strange, and important in its implications, is the finding that monkeys whose sensors were surgically removed were able after two or three months to develop a new, if somewhat less efficient, method for the task. This provides, says Bizzi:

. . . a striking example of the remarkable plasticity of the central motor apparatus, a plasticity that comes into play whenever the organism is forced to compensate for a handicap or deficit imposed on it by events over which it has no control. (p 106)

The idea of compensation is not new, but it is useful to have firm evidence for it, since this should help us to keep an open attitude, as teachers, to what the child may be able to achieve, when he has learned that he wants to learn. At about six months the child typically begins to discriminate people well enough to show fear of strangers. He sits up unaided, progresses from ham-fisted grasping to the fine movements of finger-thumb opposition, enlarges the range of food he eats as the first teeth come in. There is now a marked increase in the sounds he makes, which begin to include calls.

The baby is at the 'babbling' stage. The precise ways in which this sound producing is related to later language is not yet clearly understood. It does seem that it is during this period that the child is learning different ways in which consonant sounds are made and finding out the difference between vowel sounds and consonants. So he is discovering and applying rules to the production of sound in ways which are common to the children of many nations. 'Pappa', 'dadda', 'mamma', 'nanna' are some well known results. As specific languages are learned, the selection and differentiation of sounds must proceed, in ways which require both a sequencing of skilled motor movements and the working out of rules for putting sounds together.

The acquisition of a system for making the sounds of spoken language can be seen as intersecting with the developmental pattern involving motor and perceptual abilities. But although language usually succeeds the passing of 'motor milestones' (Lenneberg, 1967) it is not necessarily dependent upon these systems. Indeed, the acquisition of such skills as grasping, crawling, and walking will temporarily interrupt or decrease vocalizations, where the child is preoccupied with mastering such new skills.

Since there is variation in the age at which motor skills develop, and even greater individual variation in the age at which words and language are acquired, ages and stages can be widely different but still normal. It is the broad sequence of the steps which can be said to be invariant; some children may walk without going through a crawling stage, but none will walk before they can sit up. Children may articulate clearly with much or little practice in talking, but no child will speak meaningfully without going through these stages: arousal; auditory attention; the ability to identify sound, recognize its source, nature and quality; listen to the sounds he himself makes; select significant sound from background noise; attach meaning to it; and decide to respond to it with the organized motor activity of speech organs which we name as our voice.

The fact that selection of sounds-with-significance and decisions about response are already being made, underlines the social nature of even apparently elementary processes. The social influences are multiform, and show the blending of external influences and internal states. Jones (1972) summarizes the significant influences which bear on the way the child's personality, and his use of language, are developed. He includes the 'anticipatory culture' into which the child is born; the personalities and interrelations of his parents and siblings; the attitude of the parents towards the child; their theories and practices of child training; the child's own abilities, physical characteristics and health history; the opportunities he is given for recreational activities; his educational experiences; what possibilities there are for extending social contact beyond the immediate family circle; the opportunities afforded him to develop 'social maturity, self-reliance, and self-respect' (p 27).

It is in these last attributes that the child with some physical handicap is likely to miss out. It shows the need, at the baby stage, to help parents of these children with continuing support, advice and facilities, which will avoid their over-protecting their children. This over-protection can come about as a result of the parents' natural attitudes of guilt, anxiety, shame and bewilderment, which can harden into self-concealed rejection of the child if they are not enabled to come to terms with what has happened, and to set realistic but hopeful goals for the child.

From about nine months on, the process of language understanding can be seen in the child's ability to respond to simple commands which occur in a context which also gives non-auditory cues to the probable meaning: 'wave bye-bye', 'give me a bit' etc. The child also responds to 'no', but here emphasis, tone of voice and situation may carry more meaning than the word used. The rhythm and flow of sentence patterns are now rehearsed by the child through the groupings of sounds he can make into sentence-like statements and questions. These seem to convey a convincing meaning, though no individual word is recognizable. But as they are not yet used in the situations where their correct use can be assessed, it can easily and mistakenly be assumed that their practice use by the child indicates mastery of *when* they should be used.

An important parallel development is that the child is now using words with meaning. The adult regards these as one-word sentences. They are interpreted according to the situation in which they are used. 'Mummy', though frequently used, is not likely to be used just to name that indispensable person. It could mean 'I want my dinner', 'pick me up', 'give me that toy' etc. It may be differentiated into 'ninna', 'up', or 'da', according to the number, as yet small, of consonants which the child is able to couple with a vowel sound, and the words which have importance for him. Although the child is usually able to discriminate the different sounds of consonants when he hears them and can articulate up to eight, he cannot, yet, in use, manage more than one consonant in each word he says, so that his method consists either of substituting, as in 'ninna', or dropping one or both, as in 'da' for 'that', where 'the' is not yet available to him.

Getting the feedback from his own sounds through listening to them, or to the sounds others make, then repeating these and comparing them with his own sounds, or the sounds he intends to make, is vital for the change from random babbling to purposive speech. So is the adult's response to the child's efforts; language use must be seen by him as resulting in changes for the better in his environment, if he is to continue and expand its use.

Listening is in itself a complex ability, though it is only a factor in language acquisition. Murphy (1972) defines three components of focused hearing (or listening): 'These are that the attention must be focused on auditory stimuli and that the attentive focus will lead to perceptive and cognitive function.' In other words we have:

1 auditory acuity;

2 auditory attention and

3 auditory concepts.

He goes on to point out that these aspects of auditory behaviour cannot lead to language learning in the absence of a fourth and separate element; language processes. 'This is the ability to submit auditory concepts to the brain's language centres in order to develop language discrimination, comprehension and usage.' (p 95)

On our view of what happens from early childhood on, from about the time the baby has achieved the notion of the permanence of objects, which implies representational memory, a variety of features are in play together; as determinants of attention, as focussers of attention and maintainers of attention.

External situations, past knowledge, internal states, each then have their effect on this pre-language stage, just as they do on later learning.

For the deaf or partially hearing child, who lacks the first of Murphy's ingredients – auditory acuity – for listening, there are grave problems if his hearing loss is not diagnosed early. Deaf children do babble, but do not use sounds meaningfully without help. Each child has the need to hear and imitate other people's sounds, monitor his own performance through the establishment of the 'Kinaesthestic - auditory feedback loop', (the sound - sensations coming to him through his own ears) if vocalization is to continue and develop. A deaf child will turn to gesture and acquire a signing system of a symbolic type, and appears to develop 'inner language'. His system of thinking is there, using a different medium, although it may be restricted by such things as lack of social experience, and show some immaturities linked with perception problems, such as a poor body image. There may be also a late development of imaginative co-operative play.

A partially-hearing child, if not diagnosed early, is at a particular disadvantage in learning language. The sounds of speech which have the highest level of sound intensity are the vowels. These may be heard by such a child. But it is the consonants of speech, the low volume sounds, which make it easy to decipher meanings through the discrimination of speech sounds. The transition between the consonants and the vowel sounds can be shown to give most of the meaning in a sentence lacking contextual or rhythmical clues to what it says. For instance, 'u-ee' is harder to interpret than 'cm hr' (as 'come here'). A child with hearing loss often makes such good use of context and gesture cues, plus 'lip-reading' that he appears to understand what is said. But a later beginning in language, slow progress with it, and poor articulation, result. A child whose deafness is fluctuating, i.e. resulting from the effects of the respiratory infections so common in childhood, is perhaps most disadvantaged. Not only is the sound he hears less, it is distorted, and because these losses are intermittent, he adapts less well than a child with a consistent pattern of sound to attend to. Where there is also visual loss of acuity, as happens in about half of Rubella syndrome cases, it is more difficult for the child to help himself through visual communication, which would otherwise supply a great deal of supplementary information.

If the child has a 'flat' hearing loss, that is, if his loss occurs on low, medium and high frequency sounds, he can be helped fairly easily with a hearing aid, so that sound will be amplified. The commonly met with high-frequency loss, which cuts out many consonants, and parts of many sounds, can still be helped with an aid, although the aid's inability to select sound — it can only amplify — will cause some problems. The child with any considerable hearing loss has to work harder than the hearing child. Even with the best aids, training in their use, and adults who change the environment to cut down unnecessary background noise and who remember to speak close to the child, he will become more fatigued with the effort of listening, interpreting and clearly expressing language than the child who does these things without having to think about them. The effort required may be compared with that made by someone visiting a foreign country, who is hearing a second language he has some knowledge of. Here the problems of understanding lie not so much in lack of vocabulary or different grammar, but in the amount of sheer concentration needed, the difficulty of focusing the mind continually on what is being said.

Language problems of a different kind confront the child affected by the several forms of cerebral palsy. He may have difficulty in making the sequence of skilled movements required for speaking. Limited experience can also restrict the development of concepts which will help fill words with meanings. But the fact of motor difficulty does not mean that the child cannot develop understanding of language. Inner language acquisition, plus skilled help with expression and the use of alternative media for expression, plus a range of experiences, are the needs of the child with this type of handicap. With the right sort of information on what, why, and how to do it, parents may become the best therapists, especially if support and informed advice are brought to the family early, before feelings such as guilt and bewilderment have muddied over the chances of the child's handicap being accepted.

Some conditions, such as Down's syndrome, or Rubella syndrome, are often accompanied by varying degrees of visual defect and hearing loss. Down's syndrome (mongol) children also have difficulty in using their tongues in the movements needed for fluent speech. Even where the loss is slight, the combined effects are more handicapping, since they lessen the child's likelihood of being able to compensate with a different sense organ for poor level of functioning in the affected sensory system.

Taken together, then, mild physical problems must be considered as likely causes of the child's failure in spoken language and school progress. The observation of hearing loss has been confirmed in a study by Evans of 101 mongol children (Evans, 1974). The incidence of hearing loss found was 'very high'. No-one in his sample had hearing which was as good as that of the average person. Not surprisingly, the children with the greatest amount of hearing loss were found to be those most likely to use gestures instead of words; they were also the least likely to be able to understand and carry out verbal instructions.

Dr Evans does not go on to consider the effects on language acquisition of visual problems interacting with this hearing loss. Since children with short or long sight do about as well as normally sighted children at reading when their results are averaged out (Carter, 1970; Heinsen, 1970), with short sighted children tending to do rather better, medical specialists do not always appreciate that it is worthwhile to correct squints or to prescribe glasses for mild but multiple conditions.

Gaines (1970) intended to study the visual-perception development of 103 congenitally deaf American children, but found that 58% of the children also had a vision problem. She comments that it is hardly surprising that so many of the deaf children had poor sight, since the cochlea (the working part of the ear) and the retina (the light-sensitive back of the eye) are formed from the same embryonic layer, at the same stage of development. She adds:

. . . But it was surprising to find that 87% of the children whose visual defects could be corrected had not had their defects corrected. It would seem that the first work to be done for neurologically or sensory impaired children, even before perceptual or perceptual-motor training, would be checking them for optimum vision and hearing. (p 120)

Corroboration of this viewpoint comes from a study from Norway, where visual problems of children with learning difficulties were discovered. 551 children between seven and seventeen, all attending residential special schools, but none of them in schools for visually handicapped, were given thorough tests and compared with a sample from ordinary schools. The 'special' children had all had two previous sight examinations. Nonetheless, 98 children were sent for medical examination of their squints, nystagmus and other problems. Another 136 could see better when glasses were prescribed. (Krekling and Anderson, 1974. I am indebted to Mr L. Samuels for bringing this study to my notice.)

46% of the children studied in special schools had correctable visual problems, as opposed to 27% in ordinary schools. About every third child improved his visual performance with the right glasses, although about 5% still failed to reach optimum seeing levels. Some of this failure was thought to be due to 'long-term uncorrected refractive error'. Early correction of even mild conditions would help to keep up the ability to use the two eyes together for vision in depth, and for the maximum vision to be retained where there is a markedly weaker eye, as in the squints so frequently seen in Down's syndrome. As the authors say: 'Any vision problem would probably tend to deprive the individual of certain varieties of experiences that in more or less subtle ways would influence further sensory, perceptual and cognitive development.' (p 160) Some largely overlooked reasons for the markedly inferior language performance of the severely educationally handicapped, are suggested by studies such as these. They indicate the need for very early detection and treatment of eye and ear defects. It is now possible to do very much more for children who are visually handicapped for instance by removing cataracts at an early age. And an experimental method for correcting squints by showing a young baby a gingham pattern of stripes for a few minutes at a time, several times a day, giving a daily exposure of about half an hour, seems to be a promising as well as a simple technique for keeping up the binocular vision we need for full depth perception (Blakemore, 1971). If the squint is surgically corrected after the age of two, there is evidence that although the eye is then optically normal, the brain connections have been lost, through nerve degeneration. Although the ear is our main channel for learning language, a good deal of information about it, and learning relevant to its acquisition, comes to us through our sight. All that can be done to make it easier for the child to receive the maximum of information should be done.

These are examples of the way defects in perceptual and motor functions may distort or delay normal language acquisition, so that special intervention is needed to enable the child's bent for language to make itself manifest. More subtle damaging effects seem often to result from the emotional withdrawal of children who have suffered forms of deprivation such as prolonged or repeated separation from the mother in early childhood, or being 'minded' while the mother is at work, in conditions where the child has neither toys, affection, verbal stimulation, or the opportunity to explore his environment. Sometimes these children become so depressed that they refuse food, so that malnutrition is added to their other problems. Often they understand language, but are reluctant to use it. This may be coupled with an inability to show feelings either of sorrow or gladness. If they speak at all, it is often to echo adult's words in a flat, monotonous but clearly articulated way that somehow absolves them from any real participation in a verbal interchange. These children can also be helped over a period of time.

Other children, who have had severe illnesses or accidents, may have such perceptual problems, short attention span, and acute remembering problems that their language comes in only slowly. Their difficulties are specific. Other children are generally slow developmentally and begin language later, learn it more slowly. The amount of 'intelligence' required for ordinary language use is not high. Children who are generally slow to learn, acquire language in the same sequence as children who have no learning difficulties (Mittler, 1972). Braine (1971) reports a study by Lenneberg *et al* of children with Down's syndrome, which shows that 'a well-developed linguistic system is consistent with rather severe mental retardation' (p 69), and Lenneberg cites a type of dwarfism where language develops normally despite a much reduced number of brain cells.

Limited experience, deprivation, separation during hospital stays etc., anxiety, repeated failure experiences, and the interaction of these, hamper the development of retarded children. The task is objectively more difficult for them, and is made significantly more so by their secondary handicaps leading to acquired attitudes which lead them to play safe in many educational situations. There is a wealth of evidence that it is in the area of language that their retardation is most marked, often intensifying their social isolation. Even where their speech is fluent, it is often inappropriate. (See Schliefelbusch *et al* (1967) for a fuller treatment.) Yet although language is slow to develop and may not be fully used, there is no need for the teacher to accept this state of affairs as irremediable, as I hope I have shown.

Another group of children, with a quite different type of problem, also indicate that hopeful attitudes can also be realistic attitudes.

Normally - hearing children of deaf parents, if their parents 'sign', pick up sign language at about the same age as the children of hearing parents begin to talk. Hearing children of deaf parents do not seem to have unusual problems in learning to talk when they do make contact with speakers. These findings support the view of species - specific ability, based on the distinctive ways that human beings process information; it is how we interpret reality in symbolic ways. This again suggests the view that where a child's language is inadequate for his needs, widely different from acceptable norms, or apparently non-existent, there is nonetheless a basis in the child's mental equipment which, with skilled teaching, may lead to the development of the needed language skills.

The ways that children do begin to talk show some systematic differences within the general pattern of single words followed by two-word phrases. What they learn shows the importance of activity, movement and sound as well as the importance of the type of mother-response.

The way that, at about 18 months to two years, words begin to be paired together in linked concepts, can show how the differences Nelson (1973) describes alter the choices of what things are talked about, and determine how they are talked about. The vocabulary already deployed in single-word utterances is combined with another word so that it indicates more clearly the message intended. A usual example might be 'Dadda gone' or 'Mamma up'. These still need a real context, but it is one which can more readily be imagined from the sentences alone, than when just one word was used.

More idiosyncratic two-word sentences result from the child's individual characteristics. An 18 month old girl known to me had very indistinct articulation, which may have been related to the late age (13 months) at which she cut her first tooth; she also had rather poor visual acuity which led her to pay more attention to the colours of objects than to their shapes. She could recognize and indistinctly name colours, and could say 'di' for 'drink', but did not attempt to say 'milk'. So to specify what she wanted to drink, she asked for her milk as 'wha di' – 'white drink'. Thus her combination of interests, abilities, and difficulties had led her to a particular form of expression.

Alongside with these two-word sentences, and gradually

superseding them, come more complicated utterances. These have been well described by Braine (1971), who points out the frequency with which 'replacement sequences' occur. This means that the child uses first a simpler form, then, in almost the same breath, clarifies his statement by an expansion of it. Often he puts in a previously missing 'subject' as he does so. His examples (p 33) of Jonathan at 26 to 27 months show this happening:

Other coffee	Daddy other coffee
Close radio	Mommy close radio
Take off	Daddy take off. Mommy take off
Hot	Meat hot
Back there	Wheel back there etc.

Some of the consonants in the quoted examples are too difficult for most children of this age; possibly the recording adult 'heard' these in a way which also interpreted them. But the way the child struggles to make more explicit what he intends or wants, does indicate the strong motivational forces pushing the child on to more complex language forms. The two-year-old can use all the determination which marks the growing independence of the toddler stage when he insists on making his meaning clear. One such child was being pushed along a suburban street in his pushchair, when he pointed across the road, remarking to his mother as he did so, 'One on, one off.' Her absent-minded 'Yes' was evidently considered to be unsatisfactory as a reply. The child stopped the pushchair's progress by removing his feet from the step and planting them firmly on the ground. Still he pointed, and repeated 'One on, one off', with increasing emphasis.

The child's mother could see that they would stay there until the boy's meaning was discovered. Carefully looking in the direction of the imperiously pointing finger, she noticed stone gateposts flanking a garden path. One post was topped by a spherical stone. Half-hidden in the garden lay its fellow, long since fallen from its place. As the mother realized that this was what the child referred to, she replied 'Oh! Yes — one on, one off.' The child replaced his feet on the step of the pushchair, and they went on their way.

The way that an adult's instructions are carried out at the two-year-old stage can show how the child is actively processing, storing, and then re-constituting what is said into the primitive grammar which he speaks with. To return to the little girl who called her milk 'wha di' at 18 months. She had progressed to three-word sentences at two, and had invented her own private word for 'sleep', calling it 'Ooma'. When her mother instructed her to go upstairs and tell her Daddy it was time to get up, she staggered upstairs, positioned herself stragetically with her mouth to her sleeping father's ear, and bawled 'Dadda ooma gone'. She had remembered the content of the message, and delivered it through the limited grammar available to her in speech.

Grammatical structures now develop rapidly and with increasing variety. The linguists' description of this stage, when child grammar is beginning to approximate to adult grammar, but is still simple in form, is that it conforms to phrase structure rules. This means that 'transformations', which may be considered as the way simple sentences are altered into other forms, are not yet in evidence. Rules for changing word-endings according to the needs of different tenses are coming in, and are demonstrated when the child 'overgeneralizes' these rules, applying them in situations where an as yet unlearned exception is required – 'mouses', 'foots' etc.

The child's comprehension is generally agreed to be in advance of what he is able clearly to express. As we have seen, Nelson (1973) shows that good comprehension is a better indicator of a quick rate of speech acquisition than the age at which the first words are spoken.

The child's level of grammatical expression (not his understanding) is shown in the use of a primitive form of negation. 'No' or 'not' is simply added to the beginning of the sentence: 'No go bed' is used for 'don't want to go to bed'. 'Can't' is similarly expressed by 'no'. A child who could discriminate consonants far better than she could say them, so that her word 'bi' represented widely different names of things, reported to her mother that 'dadda no say bi', by which her mother could infer, from the context; that she meant to say 'Dadda can't say lid'.

These forms gradually change to such sentences as, 'That not a dog', 'Don't want some'. The absence or not-thereness of things, people, quantities, is first referred to in early statements as 'Milk gone', 'shoe gone', 'Nanna gone'. This may arise from the feeding situation, and our usual expression when the child's dinner or milk has finished: 'It's all gone', we say. In the McNeill's (1973) study of the way Japanese children come to use 'no' through the structure of their own language, this absence or disappearance seems to be the first idea of 'no-ness' to emerge in the child's thinking. It is followed by the yes/no opposition, assertion of truth or falsity, and then used for the expression of inner states of feeling, what the child does or doesn't want. McNeill's order of 'no' statements should not be regarded as exclusive or invariant – they seem to overlap considerably in English speaking children – but they provide an interesting way of looking at what is happening in the child's developing thought, as he builds up a concept of 'no' which includes a variety of specific meanings.

Question forms show a similar developmental history. The earliest forms by which a child makes an enquiry are: by a naming intonation, then probably 'Da?' or 'what dat?' Then 'Where it goes to', 'why not we can't dance?' to 'why the kitty can't stand up?' (Miller's examples quoted by Braine, 1971 p 42.)

Brown (1968) has studied how question forms increase from 'what, who, where' questions used as enquiries and the extension of these to 'why': the question teachers should never stop asking.

Cazden (1972) has compiled, from a number of sources, the ages and stages at which yes/no and wh-questioning are used. Her table includes 'tag' questions, in which a standard phrase such as 'isn't it', follows the statement and turns it into a question. (NP refers to the 'noun phrase' or 'subject' of the sentence.) (See table on p 48.)

The short sentences of the two plus period are starting to expand. So-called 'telegraphic' speech, in which only the words which carry the meaning are said, is a well-known feature which is partly explained by the fact that these 'content' words are the ones which receive the most stress in speech. The sheer difficulty of marshalling everything needed for a long spoken response may also be involved here. The way the child uses 'replacement sequences' in which he struggles to expand and thereby clarify his statements, may be a transitional stage, showing how the child might use the strategy of finding and using the most useful elements for his stage of communicative ability.

A study by Bloom *et al* (1974) shows that child learners use a learning strategy which is not necessarily the same in each case. The children who were studied varied in their amount of imitation of others' speech; a boy called Eric imitated only words he did not know, in structures which he did. Peter imitated constructions which he was just beginning to grasp, but not those which he already knew, or those which were as yet unknown. This shows that vocabulary may be used to improve grammar, or grammar to improve vocabulary.

By about three years there is approximation to adult grammar; the use of pronouns; longer sentences that give opportunities to note that the child has knowledge of rules for inflections (word-endings), and sometimes over-generalizes these; and much clearer, less idiosyncratic articulation. The child who at two used 'bi' for many objects, remarked at three 'I'm newing the bed.'

With added length and fluency comes the ability to express meanings in alternative forms. This gives us, as it develops, the opportunity to choose shades of meaning, and the personal style which comes from our choices. Clarke (1973) discusses the reasons for the three-years-six months to four-years-old child's choice of alternative ways of saying things. (For example, we can say 'He opened the door and he came in', or 'He came in after he opened the door' or 'After he opened the door he came in.') She shows that the choice is systematic, and involves three principles.

Order of mention
This includes the chronological order of events. The simplest sentence

Development of question forms

1 child: ages

		Yes-No questions	*Wh-questions*
Period A (28 mths)		Expressed by intonation only: Sit chair? Ball go?	Limited number of routines: What('s) that? Where NP go? What NP doing?
Period B (38 mths)	More complex sentences being questioned, but no development of question forms themselves, except the appearances, probably as routines, of two negative auxiliaries *don't* and *can't*	Dat black too? Mom pinch finger? You can't fix it?	What soldier marching? Where my mitten? Why you waking me up?
	Development of auxiliary verbs in the child's entire grammatical system. Inversion of aux. and subject NP in Yes-No, but not in Wh-questions	Are you going to make it with me? Will you help me? Does the kitty stand up? Can I have a piece of paper?	What I did yesterday? Which way they should go? Why the Christmas Tree? How he can be a doctor?
Period C–F (42–54 mths)		Development of tag questions from *Huh?* to mature form: I have two turn, huh? We're playing, huh? That's funny isn't it? He was scared wasn't he? Mommy, when we saw those girls they were running weren't they?	Inversion of aux. and subject NP, first in affirmative questions only: Why are you thirsty? Why can't we find the right one?
			Later, starting in Period F, negative question also: Why can't they put on their diving suits and swim?
			Development of complex questions, including indirect Wh-questions: You don't know where you're going. He doesn't know what to do. We don't know who that is.

Source: Cazden (1972)

form which can be used to describe a sequence of events is a number of single clauses. 'He opened the door. He came in.' Co-ordinate clauses, joining with 'and', also involves the events in the order of happening. 'He opened the door and came in.' But chronological order need not always determine the order of mention. Clarke points out that where the correct temporal conjunction is used, the order of events can be altered: 'He took a taxi because he missed the bus.'

Derivational simplicity
Where a choice between simpler and more complex sentence forms has to be made, the child tends to choose the one which needs the fewest 'transformations', the least amount of grammatical-rule work in it.

Choice of theme
This operates both within sentences and across them. This can give emphasis where it is wanted with a particular sentence, or provide the linking information which strings two sentences together naturally. There is obviously one 'right' pair of sentences, and one 'wrong' pair, in these examples:

'I saw a man. The man was mending a box.'

'I saw a man. The box was being mended by the man.'

Theme can be chosen independently of chronological order and derivational simplicity. In practice, a speaker's choices are limited by habitual use. It can be seen that the theme is largely dependent on the context. Clarke considers the child's ability to recognize the theme and give it its place at the beginning of the sentence may be one of the factors which precedes the learning of linguistic structures.

For the nursery age child, descriptive sentence types are acquired in the order; 'He ate and he left', 'He left after he ate', 'After he ate he left.' It would be interesting to see how the change from the first type to the second and third comes about.

Clarke recorded and analyzed the spontaneous speech of nursery school children, gaining information on the way the use of conjunctions developed as the children wanted to express temporal relations in specific ways, for which 'and' was inadequate. She found that subordinate conjunctions begin to be used at about two-years-six-months to three-years. Such terms as before, after, as, when, since, while, until, if, unless, because, are all needed to express contingency relations, and Clarke considers that the acquisition of language can be partly explained by the function of terms which meet the child's needs. Caution is needed here in interpreting the child's use of words such as 'because'. It is unlikely that his concept of the word bears much relation to adult meanings until he is at least seven. A more likely interpretation is that the child, as with 'no', expands the concept of the word he uses to express newly-understood meanings. Clarke shows that children do do this with 'and', which they first used just for joining, then to mean, 'and subsequently' and 'and previously'. The form of the sentence is thus intertwined with the child's development of such notions as 'before' and 'after'.

It is possible that the use of 'and' in these new ways helps the child to gain the concepts implied in the use of words which express a relationship in time or cause-and-effect relationships. From the newly-won concepts he might then go on to use the language terms which express them.

None of the stages of language acquisition are clear-cut or mutually exclusive. In a conversation with an adult, such primitive features as 'telegraphic' speech, and substitution of consonants, can be heard together with quite difficult constructions with correct articulation. Sometimes these occur in the same conversational interchange, sometimes they can be observed over a period of time, as in the following examples.

A two-year-old boy who had a bad dream whispered to himself, 'Nuffink will get me', and later enquired of his mother, 'Where likkle animals, Mummy?' She asked him which animals. 'Likkle animals in bedroom.' On hearing that there were no little animals, that it was 'only a dream' the child laughed heartily, replying, 'Oh! Thought likkle animals were going to eat me up.'

Some weeks later another dream; in the morning the child looked resignedly at his hands, saying. 'No fumbs, no fumbs' – then adding in surprise, 'Oh! I dreamed my fumbs were down to there' (indicating joint).

So words which he had learned early, like 'thumbs', continued to have a substituted sound, but the later addition to his vocabulary, 'thought', was rendered correctly (see first example).

By about four, the child is using more complex sentences, with embedded clauses. There is some disagreement amongst linguists about the understanding and use of passive constructions. Campbell and Wales (1970) have pointed out that an absence of passive sentences may be attributable either to lack of capacity, or absence of occasions for their production. Relevant situations are needed for the observation of whether many structures are present in the child's competence. For instance, Campbell and Wales report a study where pre-school Edinburgh children were shown cardboard soldiers of varied size. Some of the structures used by the children to describe them included absolute terms – 'He's big', comparatives – 'He's bigger than him' etc., superlatives – 'He's the biggest soldier', as well as 'functional' comparisons – 'He's too big', 'He's wee enough' etc.

Pre-school children interpret words in ways we should be aware of when we ask them to carry out 'Piagetian' tasks such as classification or conservation. Nursery school children who were shown model trees on which they could hook apples, tended to respond to, 'Make it so there are less apples on this tree than on this one' in the same way as they did to a similar sentence substituting 'more' for 'less'. And in classifying 'the same as' is often interpreted in the same way as is 'different from'. The fact that a child has in his vocabulary terms which can be used in thinking (see Clarke's study) and in reasoning, does not mean that he is making use of them as in adult concepts. When he asks 'why' or says 'because' he may still be far from the idea of causal relationships. 'When' does not mean he has a realistic notion of time, though the use of these terms may be helping him through a transitional stage.

Nor does the development of articulation, with more difficult consonants and clusters of consonants being incorporated into the increasing flow of speech, always proceed smoothly. As Ingram (1972) points out, it is just at this two-years-six-months to four-years-old stage that hesitations, stammers and stutters frequently occur. In most cases it is a passing phase, but is likely to be accentuated or even perpetuated if parental reaction to the symptoms lead to the child becoming sensitive and consequently anxious about his 'non-fluency'.

The child has many developmental steps still to take, but he has now acquired mobility of movement and action, and ways of using perceptual abilities such as sight and hearing to explore his environment; when he was largely dependent on touch he had to be close to objects to investigate their properties. He has a store of knowledge which he can enlarge not only through actions and perceptions but with the new dimensions of language. He has new ways of experiencing and mastering reality through play experience.

A very readable account of play at the nursery school age by Cass (1971) discusses play at five developmental stages. First there is solitary play with toys or things he pretends with, followed by spectator play, in which children are watching each other, then parallel play, where they like to be near each other, associative play, where they appear to be playing together, and finally cooperative play. Different types of play and games require a differing amount and quality of talk among the participants. Groups come together, change, break up; temporary leading figures change in the process of role-making and role-taking; children talk apparently to themselves but decrease their talk when they are alone (Vygotsky, 1962); these are play stages typical of the three to five-year-olders.

They are in themselves such an incentive to the child to develop language that they may well be connected with the observations that show how children of nursery school age use more complex sentences at the five and four-year-old level, that is the age when cooperative play is becoming established, than at three, and that their language use is more sustained when they start talking to their friends than it is when the teacher starts a conversation with the child. This tends to confirm Campbell and Wales' point that certain sources of linguistic information — the adult's utterances which give language examples to the child — may have been overvalued by linguists, who discuss it as the only information about language available to the child. They suggest that the communicative environment, the feedback which the child gets from what he says in his interaction with people, is an important source of information to him about whether what he has said is understandable and appropriate to the occasion. If it is both of these, he gets what he wanted, or finds out what he wanted to know.

This again connects with the need to develop patterns of attentive behaviour, of experimentation with social roles and emotional attitudes, of evaluating these in the light of social reactions, and adopting or rejecting them as part of behaviour and of the developing personality (Murphy, 1972). Murphy makes the further important point that the notion of the child's pleasure through the feedback he receives is hardly tenable if the home situation is ignored. There is a particular need to involve the child's mother if his language is delayed. As Murphy says:

The child who is prevented from communicating adequately not only suffers from frustrations commonly recognized and acknowledged by therapists but is deprived of a basic need, a source of comfort and security and, perhaps most important, a source of self-expression and therefore of the feedback process which underlies the development of self-realization and self-identification. Without these two last qualities, the mechanism by which a child recognizes his own existence and social function may be so severely impaired as to prevent any real social contact or manipulation of the real environment. (p 101)

The nursery-age children have also made discoveries about their language, not easily explained by transformational grammar, such as the correct placing of adjectives. We speak of 'a black, nasty, dirty, damp, decrepit old house', or 'an old house, decrepit, black, dirty, nasty, damp', according to whether we are speaking naturally or creating a self-conscious literary effect. What we somehow reject would be 'a damp, black, old, decrepit, dirty, nasty house'. Even a young child would speak of 'a little old man' rather than 'an old little man'. The child at this age is unused to the breakdown of the sentence into individual words, because he is unfamiliar with their written forms; so a three-year-old child by an ice-cream van, asked by her mother if she wanted a big one or a small one, replied 'I'd like a nice big cream.' She showed both that she usually thought of this desirable commodity as 'a nice cream', and also that she knew the adjective of size came nearer to the noun in this case. Yet adjective order is hardly a reflection of 'deep' grammatical rule, more of a customarily met with collocation (or string) of words. It seems possible to explain this as a preference learned by experience of what 'feels' right. By the age of five most children do have a remarkable amount of such language with which they handle a range of situations.

If all has gone well, the child of this age has acquired the main rules of the grammar of his language; these will be refined and added to as his general ability increases in the 'concrete operational' stage described by Piaget. He still has to expand his vocabulary a great deal, on the basis of widening experience and knowledge. The more difficult strings of consonants, as in 'crisps', still need perfecting, and babyish substitutions of the 'likkle', 'miggle' type often still have to be replaced. The primitive concepts which he has about the meanings of words, such as the early notion of treating 'same as' and 'different from' as if they carried the same meaning, have to be brought in line with adult usage. The word gradually has to be dissociated from the thing it refers to, unlinked from the characteristics of the object it names. The notion of word-play, jokes based on alternative meanings, comes as the child is able to appreciate more than one point of view. Even the ability to tell a lie has to be based on a clear sense of what is real and what is fantasy, or 'only dreaming', and so marks a stage of language ability.

The vocabulary used by children is expanded by particularization and generalization. The word 'flower' becomes particularized into 'buttercup', 'daisy', 'tulip' etc., 'dog' to 'horse', 'cow', 'sheep'. 'Father' becomes one particular adult, though the use of this 'strict' form instead of the familiar 'dad' may lead the child, whose mother threatens him, 'Just wait, I'll tell your Father', to enquire, 'What, our Father wot art in Heaven or our Dad?' There is a great growth of vocabulary between six and eight. Besides the increasing number of words used in children's free writing there is an increasing tendency for the widening of concepts to find its expression in more generalized terms chosen by the child: 'house' is superseded by 'home'.

The refinement of vocabulary to express a thought or feeling as precisely as possible can be helped by introducing children to poetry. They can learn to make it themselves, often first through the security of the group, then progressing to their own individual style, the route particular to them. This ability is not limited to children living in our better suburbs. A class of six-year-olds in an educational priority area, comprising children of West Indian, Asian, Irish, Greek Cypriot and Birmingham parentage provides examples. The first two are group work (put together from a number of suggestions volunteered by the class members around a theme selected by the teacher). These are followed by some individual compositions.

Put a book silently on the table
Tiptoe upstairs
Whisper to a little boy
Just quietly.

The flower smells gorgeous
Sweet like cakes and lemonade
Petals curved like a bell
It's a hyacinth.

Penelope wrote:

Flowers come back because we want Christmas roses
We like to see some
Flowers in the garden
Look to the left and you will see some roses.

Her twin brother Odesseaus wrote:

I caught a snake the other day
I caught it in my hand
It jumped up and fell on my head.

Jasvinder wrote:

Roses bloom in the summer
I like the smell of roses
I love roses.

Elaine, withdrawn, depressed and undernourished, obscurely stated:

Cats and dogs are going up to the moon
Children saying Good-bye
Girls and boys are saying good-bye.

But Louis' bounce and exuberance came through with:

The sun shines through the window
I jump out of bed
I feel glad
I wish I were a dog
So I could run fast.

The 'wish I were' construction, or similar examples such as 'I would like', 'You should sit still', which convey a sense of the difference between the actual and the ideal, were frequently used by these children, including those who, because of immigration, had acquired their English only recently. Mohammed, for instance; I had a cough, and Mohammed, politely waving his hand for permission to speak, observed: 'Miss, you should go to the doctor's.' When he had considered my reply, to the effect that if I did so the doctor would tell me to go to bed, whereas I wanted to come to school to teach him, he offered me an alternative: 'Miss, you can buy bottles of cough mixture for grown ups from the chemist.' Language can now be used to think out the solution of a problem.

There are different interpretations of the nature and purpose of young children's use of 'egocentric' speech. Piaget found that a large proportion of speech had no apparent communicative intent, since the child, talking only about what he is doing, does so without expecting answers or being influenced by what others are saying. He does not seem to mind if no-one is listening to him. The lesser part of the speech of children under seven is 'socialized' in the sense of asking for and giving information in answer to the questions of others, and so on. This led Piaget to call the larger part of the young child's speech 'egocentric'.

'Egocentric' speech is said to subside and fade out at the age of seven or eight when social behaviour is becoming more established. Vygotsky (1962) challenged Piaget's belief that egocentric speech does not fulfil any realistically useful function for the child and that it therefore dies out. To test this, Vygotsky notes changes in the child's 'monologue' while he is carrying out some activity. In very young children he studied, it marked the end of the activity. Then it moved towards the middle of the activity. Finally, it preceded it to give purpose, intention, planning, to the child's activity. Vygotsky looks on 'egocentric' speech as a transitional stage In between that of older children, who tackled problems in silence. When asked what they were thinking about, they showed by their replies that their thoughts had similarities with 'egocentric' speech. Vygotsky sees the stages of the child's use of language as social speech, then egocentric speech, followed by inner speech. This contrasts both with the behaviourist stages of vocal speech, whisper, inner speech; and Piaget's stages of non-verbal thought, egocentric thought and speech, socialized speech and 'logical' thinking.

The differences in these models of Vygotsky and this early work of Piaget, which he has since modified, are reflected in their models of the child's way of thinking. Piaget's non-operational, pre-operational, concrete operational and formal operational model has become familiar to educators. Vygotsky shows some measure of agreement in his own four stages. First, a primitive stage which corresponds to the infant's pre-intellectual speech and his non-verbal thoughts expressed in the manipulation of objects. Second, 'naive psychology', experience of himself and his surroundings as applied to the use of tools. This corresponds with the stage of the child's use of correct grammatical forms before their relations are grasped. Third, external operations to solve internal problems, as in counting on fingers. Fourth, the 'ingrowth' stage characterized by the use of logical memory, and the interaction between outer and inner operations.

Vygotsky considers that the child who cannot yet fully understand the word in an adult way, can often have sufficient experience shared between himself and the adult for the 'meeting' or understanding of each other to take place; this tends to mislead the adult into thinking that the child's concepts are the same as his. Vygotsky calls this stage of child thinking 'pseudo-concepts'. He also distinguishes 'complex formation' and 'potential concepts'.

True concepts are seen as demanding not just the abstraction of traits, but their new synthesis through the mediating action of the word, 'deliberately used to direct all the part processes of advanced concept formation' (p 78).

Because five and six-year-old children have mastered the most used sentence forms, it would be easy to assume as some linguists, e.g. McNeill, have done that language development is complete. The few available studies (Carol Chomsky; Kessel, 1970) reveal areas where this is not so.

Some sentences have to be understood by the listener making an assumption about who is meant to be the 'subject' of what is happening. Thus, in the sentence 'John asked Bill to leave', we interpret the meaning as showing that Bill is to be the one to leave. In the sentence 'John told Bill to leave', we have to make a similar assumption. This can be generalized into the rule that in this type of sentence, the person (Bill) who is named closest to the infinitive verb (leave) is to be regarded as the subject of the action. But the English language here reveals a deficiency in its vocabulary. The verb 'to ask' has to cover for two different uses. Sometimes ask is used as 'request', sometimes in the sense of 'question'. For instance, Kessel cites the sentences 'John asked Bill what to do' and 'John told Bill what to do.' The rule which worked with the previous pair of sentences still works with the new sentence 'John told Bill what to do' which clearly means he told Bill what he, Bill, should do. It is not so with the other sentence, 'John asked Bill what to do', which means that John asked Bill what he, John, ought to do. Previous research had shown the child's tendency to over-generalize rules of plurals and tenses ('mices', 'I seed', 'I'm newing the bed'), learning exceptions later. So Carol Chomsky, and later Kessel, investigated middle-class children of average ability to find the age at which most children correctly deal with this exception. Kessel found that seven-year-olds had a low error rate; that almost all eight-year-olds succeeded, and all nine-year-olds did. (C. Chomsky's exploratory study showed ten as the usual age.)

If this helps to show how slowly some exceptions to rules are learned, even more can be learned from the study of how children interpret 'ambiguous' sentences.

There are three types of sentences in which more than one meaning can be discerned. One is by a play of word-meaning: 'The soldiers liked the port.' Another involves two distinct possible groupings of adjacent words; it is an ambiguity of surface structure: 'Small boys and girls are frightened easily.' This is in fact more ambiguous when written down, since the spoken version by intonation, stress and pauses, would be likely to indicate whether 'small' is grouped only with 'boys', or is to be taken to qualify 'boys and girls'. The third type of ambiguity involves the deep structure, the logical relations between words and phrases: 'The Mayor will ask the police to stop drinking.' Here the logical relations between 'police' and 'drinking' determine who it is who should stop. The meaning of individual words remains the same, nor is their grouping altered according to which meaning is perceived.

Kessel found, using Piagetian questioning methods to test his subjects' understanding of that interpretation of the test materials, that six and seven-year-olds could detect the word-meaning ambiguities. The surface structure ambiguities were much harder; nine-year-olds showed a marked improvement. Only his twelve-year-olds showed a consolidated proficiency. With the even harder underlying ambiguities, he only got consistently correct comprehension in twelve-year-olds. Only these made spontaneous comments of the type which indicated that their thinking was at the level of 'formal operations' e.g. 'You can look at it differently', 'It depends on the way you phrase it.'

In our day-to-day conversational exchanges it also depends on the context, which usually gives us a clear indication of which meaning we are to select for perception. The six and seven-year-olds' success with alternative word meanings is connected with the pleasure with which this age group engages in verbal play: riddles, jokes, puns, games of the 'knock, knock who's there' type where skills are practised. The surprise effect of the new meaning perceived in the old word consolidates concepts which have been building up through earlier development stages.

The later growth of a sure ability to perceive more than one logical relation in a sentence (when there is no help received from contextual clues) is reflected in another language ability not considered by Kessel. The young child cannot perceive or understand metaphorical meanings in sentences or stories; his interpretation is literal. He cannot consider it as implying a deeper and different meaning in a context altered from the one he encounters it in. Thus the high incidence of metaphor in 'Black' English can be taken to indicate that this variant demands a high level of abstract thinking ability in speaker and listener.

The ability to comprehend is developing throughout childhood. There is no moment when a child 'understands' fully everything which he makes use of, or uses everything he can understand. In this, language ability can be compared with the child's mixed ability at conversation tasks during the concrete-operational period. The child does not even freely use the word separated fully from the object it refers to. Vygotsky (1962) reports discussions with children in which he proposed to call a dog a cow. The interchange shows how linked are characteristic features of the animal with its name in childish thought:

'Does a cow have horns?'
'Yes.'
'But don't you remember that the cow is really a dog? Come now, does a dog have horns?'
'Sure, if it is a cow, if it's called cow, it has horns. That kind of dog has got to have little horns.' (p 58)

Piaget has shown how children can use words like 'because' and 'although' without real understanding. A seven and nine-year-old could both conclude a sentence with '. . . because . . .' The seven-year-old could not define it. Even at nine years of age it is difficult for the child to explain the meaning of because; 'It's the word that comes — that comes — its usually before you say the reason for a thing' was the answer of the highly verbal nine-year-old child. It can be quite illuminating to ask junior children to conclude a sentence such as, 'The boy went to school, although . . .'

Even more complications occur in interpreting dictionary meanings of words so that the nearest corresponding concept is selected by the child to get a fit between thought and word.

Written language imposes its own conditions. Since it will be read in the absence of its original context, it forces the use of 'abstract' terminology on the child. He has to use expanded descriptive forms to make his meaning clear. As Greenfield et al (1966) put it:

. . . all of the semantic and syntactic features . . . become necessary when one must communicate out of the context of immediate reference. It is precisely in this respect that written language differs from the spoken . . . (p 225)

This is what Bernstein has called 'elaborated code' and 'universalistic' meanings. According to Greenfield's interpretation, any written language used out of a concrete context should produce the same cognitive results.

As well as this, the child has to sort out sentences into their separate spaced elements of words that are groups of letters (cf. the common error of a child writing 'another' as 'a nother'). He has to come to terms with reasonably correct spelling and grammar. He has to use punctuation to represent the rhythms of speech patterns. And he has to achieve this without the aid of the feedback he would get from another person's response in conversation – 'Yes, I see', grunt, 'Oh', etc., without the use of his own verbal emphasis, facial expression, gesture, body movement, tone of voice, or speed of delivery. He has to learn, in making written accounts of factual experiences, to use a tone that is neutral, objective, impersonal, yet switch readily to a lesser formality, a more individual route for expressive writing.

Luria (1960) has also concentrated on speech as a conceptual tool, an initiator of actions, and later in the child's development, as a means of stopping an unwanted action. His studies of this are open to a variety of criticisms on methodological grounds, on the type of situation he tested children in, and his limited view of what language is best used for. However, the general conclusions of Vygotsky and Luria of how their work might be applied to teaching seem more fruitful. They propose that instead of assessing a child by what he can do, we should compare the child's performance of a given task with how well he performs the task with adult help. The amount of use which he can make of this help, the effectiveness with which he can apply this to his own independent activity, could then be the basis for the assessment of his ability. 'With help today, alone tomorrow' describes quite well much of the aims and method in teaching.

As the child explores his world, he seeks out new places and events as objects of his attention and curiosity, imposing order on this raw experience by selecting, condensing and absorbing what he conceives of as relevant to his needs, desires and intentions. So what he notices depends not only on outside things which reinforce his impressions, but his own state of body and mind, his own attitudes.

On this view, all areas of human functioning are more complex than any stimulus-response conditioning model allows for. Central processes within the brain now appear to be involved in all motor and perceptual tasks as well as in thinking and feeling.

The theory of relativity has resulted in enormous changes in physics; its standpoint that what happens is relative to the viewpoint of the observer is used as an analogy in some psychological thinking.

It is from this approach that we get the argument that sources of pleasure, and therefore of reinforcement, are relative, (Kagan, 1967) and that the essence of learning is dependent on arousal, on getting the learner's attention and involving him in the process, using changes in stimulation appropriate to the child's experience and knowledge.

Surprise, an amount of uncertainty, the familiar that is made sufficiently novel to encourage its exploration by the child, (Hunt, 1961) the pleasure of recognition of the old in a new form, become important when the child is considered as 'a cognitive creature who is attempting to put structure or create schema for incoming stimulation' (p 141).

It is in this way that we have considered what happens during the time a child begins to learn language. As we have seen, it means a shift to recognition of the way learning is affected by the learner himself; his past experiences; the external situation; his internal state; what he already knows as a determinant of what he pays attention to; his feelings about himself and about other people; the situation he is in; his needs; how he applies all that is in the past to the present task of organizing actions, perceptions, images, symbols, and how he then synthesizes these, absorbs them, taking them into experience and memory. It means considering how to supply each such learner with the situations, materials and methods which enable that particular person to learn.

In one sense, language is never fully developed, since the individual's use of his native tongue should grow and change with him, not only until he has reached adult stature, but throughout his whole life. Cazden (1972) has considered this growth under three headings; learning how, learning that, learning to. In 'learning how', she considers that if the user takes care of the functions of what he wants to express, then the form will take care of itself. In 'learning that', we acquire our own 'mental dictionary', which catalogues our personal knowledge of the world. In 'learning to', enjoyment of language is the keynote, leading to purposeful control over its use.

4

Socialization and language use

The study by Nelson (1973) of the ways in which children learn to talk, has provided us with insights into the way maternal styles affect the rate of development of early words and sentences. Her study of the children of white American middle-class families found that where mothers accepted their child's attempts at speech, were non-directive towards his play, and did not attempt to control his own efforts to form concepts about the world, the children's language developed more quickly. In families where the child's attempts were criticized or ignored, and direction of his behaviour was the rule, ('Do it this way – no, don't bang the doll') the child's rate of language acquisition was slowed down. Nelson discusses how the mother's style may affect later learning. She believes that the greater the mother's control, the more restricted the range of concepts that the child will learn. The process of parental education is thus seen as persuading the child that his own categories are not to be trusted, and that he must rely on parents, and later on teachers and scholars, to define the world for him (p 118).

This finding is similar to that of Miller (1971). He discusses factors which adversely affect a child's school progress and which cut across social class boundaries. One of the family types most likely to lead to lack of school success is one where the parents are authoritarian in their control, and where this attitude is accepted by the child himself.

So the type of family the child grows up in, how he becomes 'socialized', is important for his language development and his attitudes. Socialization is a word frequently met with, yet its meaning is so wide that it could be meaningless unless an attempt is made to define its use. It refers to processes by which the infant and child is led to take unto himself the way of life of his family; this is often called primary socialization. Then, in secondary socialization, he learns to relate to the larger social groups to which he will belong. For to be accorded full adult status, he will have to relate to, and perform at, certain acceptable levels, depending on the values and goals he has acquired.

The initial provision of nurture, protection, and stable relationships with loving persons who give attention and stimulation, establish a child's basic trust; this is a motivating force in his efforts to acquire physical, cognitive, and social skills. Language and his sense of himself develop, and not just through explicit forms of communication. Facial expressions, gestures etc., are also means whereby the appraisal of others can be incorporated into the sense of self. Language has an important part to play as personality develops.

Most of the many studies of the socialization process have centred on the developmental aspect I have briefly described. They have asked questions concerning how examples of adults' standards of behaviour become part of the child's way of thinking (internalization of norms); how particular skills come about, how personality develops, and, more recently, on the growth of language skills. Following Erikson (1965) attention has been given to the developmental stages of early personality development. These were regarded by Erikson as the growth of patterns of mutual relations between the self and others, involving conflict at each stage. Developing to the next stage involves overcoming the conflict between trust/distrust, confidence/ doubt, initiative/guilt. The tasks of childhood change both according to growing abilities and the needs and demands of the society lived in and to be worked in.

Another aspect of the study of socialization has been the search for the antecedents of the adult personality traits 'dependency' and 'aggression' in child-rearing practices. Danziger (1971) points out that the weakness of this approach lies in the fact that these categories of adult human behaviour that so often provide the starting point for the earlier studies of socialization are essentially definitions of current social problems. He considers this as a lack of a deeply-thought theoretical basis leading to over-generalized conclusions, and to the ignoring of the effect of different situations on alleged personality traits.

This situational effect is well known to teachers. For example, when a group of children is taken camping, the child who is a 'nuisance' in class is often the one who is most helpful, cheerful or resourceful in facing difficulties which occur.

Danziger (1971) states that 'growing dissatisfaction' with the old type of research study, the few consistent findings which relate childhood experiences to adult behaviour, has turned some investigators to the study of socialization as a process rather than as an effect. This approach focusses more on the longitudinal studies of individuals over a period of time, and the changing patterns of their personality and behavioural characteristics.

Yet another approach is suggested by Speier (1970) who proposes to set aside questions of the child's development, while retaining adult-child and child-children interaction as central features of the process. He defines socialization as 'the acquisition of interactional competences' (p 189), and studies these as they occur in everyday activities. This involves analysing the talk through which communication mainly takes place. By thinking about conversational exchanges, as they occur in a particular situation on a particular occasion, Speier hopes to discover key facts of children's thinking. He illustrates this in the way that a child may ask another child's mother if her boy can come out to play; or how a child discovers which people are members of his family, and not just family friends; or how a search for a 'systematic procedural basis' in family interactions may be made from studying the different forms of naming which are applied to family members.

Each child born into a family unit — that is, into a socially defined situation — has much to learn about the ways the people in it behave to each other. He has to learn about attitudes, habits, values, norms of living. Contrast this with the baby's first reactions. These are undifferentiated and involuntary reflexes he is born with, which he cannot help displaying in certain set situations. He cries, smiles, makes bodily movements, which call forth a maternal protective response in whoever is looking after him. As his brain rapidly develops, and as he learns what to expect from what happens around him, these primitive systems are superseded. It is now thought that even in the earliest weeks after birth, the baby is responding to his environment in a way that indicates selection of experience is taking place. This is always a difficult thing to be sure of, since the young child has so little control over his bodily responses to things that interest him. But in an ingenious study, Mills and Melhuish (1974) show that four-week-old babies prefer to hear their mother's voice to a stranger's voice. Mothers can tell their own baby's cry two or three days after his birth.

Visual abilities also seem to be developing earlier than we used to think possible; by two months the child can certainly be said to be an active agent in his own learning. If he is shown patterns, he can stop looking at them when their repeated presentation becomes boring to him. Patterns which resemble faces always seem to interest him more than non-faces, though he responds first to parts rather than to the whole face.

In his interactions with other people, the child learns too to know which sensations come from inside his own body, and which come from outside himself. Even to recognize that there is an 'inside' and an 'outside' requires considerable knowledge, represents an important step in the process of we name as 'socialization'. This process can hardly be understood as a one-way process in which the adult activates a response in the passive imitating child.

The child's individual reactions to his mother affect her attitudes, and therefore her handling of the child. This back-and-forth relationship results in parents acting differently with different children within the same family; even with the same child at different ages. As Danziger (1971) puts it: '. . . parent and child form a system in which both partners control and socialize each other and both are dispensers of rewards and sources of information.' (p 63)

This is now recognized as applying to the 'autistic' child. At one time there was a belief that the difficulties of this type of child were 'caused' by a cold and unresponsive mother; now the effect on the mother of the child's lack of response is taken into account.

But mother-child interaction is still over-simplified as a scheme. The role of the father and of the peer group is also important for the child's development into a normal adult. So it might be more accurate to consider the social situation as a quartet of contrapuntal relationships rather than a solo melodic theme. Kagan (1967) in a plea for us to accept the idea that behaviour, because it rests on internal processes, is necessarily ambiguous, points out that it is not just the parental behaviour, which varies widely across different cultures, but what the child makes of this that is important. Rejection or acceptance by the parent is seen as 'a belief held by the child; not an action by a parent' (p 137). So if a mother slaps her child on very slight provocation, it need not mean more than a social variation in socializing techniques. The mother believes that physical punishment should be applied by a loving parent to socialize the child and prevent him from growing up to be 'a bad boy'.

Thus social variation, plus congenital and environmental difference in the responsiveness of infants, work together; but from the body of experience around him, the child manages to abstract rules for living with people. Understanding grows between them. Their responses to each other become appropriate.

There are but few well substantiated cases of children whose early years have been spent in extreme social isolation. Davis (1949) makes a comparison between two children seen by him. Anna was kept isolated in an upstairs room, with the bare minimum of physical care, until nearly six years of age. Davis describes her condition when she was found:

She was completely apathetic, lying in a limp, supine position and remaining immobile, expressionless and indifferent to everything. She was believed to be deaf and possibly blind. She of course could not feed herself or make any move in her own behalf. (p 205)

Anna died four and a half years later, and by that time she could walk well, run clumsily, 'follow directions', talk 'in phrases', repeat words and try to carry on a conversation. She could keep herself clean, and she tried to help other children.

Isabelle was found at six and a half years of age. She also had been secluded and, for much of the time, kept in a dark room. But not alone. Her mother, a deaf-mute, spent most of her time with Isabelle, who seems to have acquired a natural signing system instead of spoken language. (See Cicourel for a discussion of the difference between 'native' signing and signing acquired as a second language.) She is reported as resembling a deaf child in many of her actions, and showed extreme fear and hostility towards strangers. She was pronounced 'feeble-minded' and wholly uneducable, but a 'systematic and skilful program of training' was begun. This resulted, after the initial difficulties were overcome, in Isabelle making the equivalent of six years of educational progress in just two years. By eight and a half she was normal and went to school (p 207).

Davis discusses their different improvement rates, suggesting the possibility that Anna had less innate capacity than Isabelle. This may or may not be so, but it seems unlikely that it was the only factor involved. Comparisons may make this clearer. Dennis and Dennis (quoted by Hunt 1961), cite orphanage children in Teheran. By the age of two years, only 40% of these were sitting up alone, and only 15% walking by the age of four plus. These children were said to be of normal potential, physically well looked after, but in a situation where they were drastically deprived of stimulating experiences, as well as having few human contacts. And White (1971) has shown the opposite; that young babies can learn looking up, reaching for, and grasping an object at an earlier age than is usual, by increasing the stimulating play objects available to them. These opportunities to see and hear many things may develop readiness for activities which at first sight don't seem related to the earlier experience.

This is something which may seem surprising, particularly as it used to be thought that 'readiness' for such tasks as stair climbing, or building towers with blocks, could not be induced by practice; maturation was thought to be a function of a process of intrinsic growth. The observation, for instance, that the swaddled babies of Hopi Indians, when unwrapped from their swaddling bands, crawled at a normal age, and that one twin who was given stair climbing practice climbed no earlier than the unpractised twin, seemed to lead to this conclusion. But it is now considered that this did not take into account the effect of experiences apparently, but only apparently, unrelated; the sights, sounds, touch, smell, taste of the world around. It has been shown with animals that the ability to solve problems when adult varies according to the quality of their early experiences, and that higher animals show a greater amount of variation; for instance, Thompson and Heron (quoted Hunt, 1968) found that pet-reared dogs were better than cage-reared dogs at solving problems.

To return to Isabelle, it does seem that her chances were greatly improved by the companionship of her mother and the fact that she was thus able to learn a symbolic system (sign language) with which to organize the severely restricted events around her. Thus the learning of language, with her sentences coming only two months after the first vocalizations, with her reading and writing beginning only nine months after that, could proceed at the accelerated rate that it did. She had been secluded but, unlike Anna, she had had interaction with a loving adult, and had developed some of her latent human capacity. But Anna had been so isolated and so extremely deprived that when she was found she displayed no 'intelligent' behaviour. She helps to show firstly that there cannot be an unsocialized person, since it is through socialization that the ability to become a person is realized, and secondly that a symbolic system of communication is important for the socialization process.

The symbolic system we most frequently use is language. Through its use the child acquiring language learns that the label 'mummy' or 'daddy', at first widely applied, is used to denote particular people. He learns that these people can be referred to by other names too: Auntie, Ellen, Mrs ——, father, Uncle, Grandad. One of the signs of the child who is in 'care' can be the way he calls all adults 'Matron' or 'Auntie'. He has not had the experience of hearing people addressed by a variety of naming words. He is limited in his understanding of them, in that he does not see them behaving differently to different people at different times. Without knowledge of formal/informal, businesslike/playful, efficient/exploratory modes of behaviour, he lacks the materials through which he can form and test in action, ideas of what behaviour is appropriate. A child who approached the educational psychologist with the greeting 'Hallo my darling', was thought to be cheeky, when in fact he just did not know that in this context it was not suitable. He is not of course the only person whose attempt to break the ice, in a situation of felt strain, has fallen flat.

As the child learns to read and write, his means of finding his place in life may alter from play activities and conversations, through story listening and story telling, to story writing. Place in the family expands to place in the larger society. The child's dependence on adults moves to the need to be accepted by other children. Yet he still has the same need to believe that his own family's ways of doing and saying things is right. Any conflict between home values and school values should be minimized.

Some of the joys, uncertainties and fears which beset children at points where they are growing to a new stage are expressed through drawings and writings in terms of fantasy and dream. It is a form of thinking by analogy, which, at a much later stage, is lifted into conscious use in metaphor. The young child uses it with all the freedom of unawareness. For the teacher it can be all the more enlightening in its unconscious revelation of the child's inner world.

Working out how to get along with other people is one of the concerns of seven-year-olds which may be expressed within the written framework of 'Once upon a time'.

Once upon a time there was a cat and a rabbit and he live in a hol and one day the Rabbit went far a wuck and he met a cat and the cat hit the Rabbit and the Rabbit went and fesht his Father and his Father hit the cat (and the cat) fesht his Father and the to Father stded to fiting and las they mad frends and the cat mad Frends with the Rabbit.

Once upon a time ther was a boy and girl and the boy gave the girl a pigey back and the boy fell over a ston and he cutet his leg and the girl sede how bid you bo it sowe the boy sede you made me dow it the girl sede I neve made you dow it sow The doy sede sorey I neve ment it and made frens.

Adventure, a beginning of sketching the themes of what it is like to feel a person independent of family and teachers, yet still in need of authority figures when danger becomes too threatening, is explored in this six and a half-year-old boy's story.

Once upon a time there lived a boy and one day in the summer he went to the sea-side When he got there he went down to the beach on beach he saw some cliffs and on the cliffs there was a cave and in the lived some pirates he climbed up the cliffs to the cave when he got to the cave he went inside the cave and they caught him they went to another part of the cave but the boy broack away and jumped from the cave to the beach he changed into his swimming costume and he dived into the water he swam and, he swam and then he saw a tresher chest he caught it up and looked inside it and there was tresher there inside he shut the lid got hold of the handle and swam back when he had got back and was by the cliffs again Ther the pirates jumped down on him the police herd them they arrested the pirates in the end the pirates were hanged.

Two weeks later, the same child's story portrays the hero reaching his own solutions to the problems life poses. Repetitive phrases such as 'every time' are used to replace the emphasis gained by stress in spoken language, and much of the phraseology is much nearer to spoken than written forms. It is clearly not a story retold from memories of a story read to him, although the Elks in 'Sweedon' are remembered from a story. He has also now adopted the bookish convention of 'The end'.

Once upon a time there lived a hunter every time he went out hunting he shot two birds one dear three fox's and four wolf's every time but when he was out hunting he shot ten of every animal in the forest but one day he didn't shoot any animals so he chached his job he chached it to a builder but they didn't want him so he went to Sweedon. When he got there he went strait to the big forest which he could see to hunt Elkes he hunted all that day he never stoped hunting til he saw that he had realy a shoc he had been hunting for twenty four hours so he went back to the airport Just in time to catch the aireplane but he landed in India so he got on the right plane at least he thought it was but it floo right on to iland so he had to go back to England by ship on the realy right ship he hunted in the forest that he hunted in before every time he hunted in that forest, and he lived happly ever after. The end.

The theme of how to cope may be entwined with and absorbed by the felt need to belong within a family. A six-year-old girl's story exemplifies this, in a story she calls 'The boy who lived by himself'.

Once upon a time lived a little boy. He lived in a house by himself one day there was no food left what can I do will be parkeeper when he had got lots of money what a lot he did have sispences pennies and shillings but by now he was starved and it was past the day So he ran and ran and ran untill he came to a shop he went in he said to the lady may I have a pound of potatoes and some nice meat and 3 carots and peas he paid his money and ran home he cooked it all up and eat it up suddenly there was a tat-a-tat-tat at the door then the little boy ran to the door at the dor stood Mr Fox help help help called him but how could he get out of the house to run? the fox got him But the fox carried him away he went to his den help help help but nobody heard the fox was sharpening his knife but a little elephant he saw the foot-prints and and followed them untill he came to the foxes hole and banged at the door it went opened he put down his trunk the little boy got on it and the Elephant pulled him up the little boy ran and ran home but the Elephant called but he ran on untill a lady stoped him do you no who was calling for help Yes said the little boy I was me wear you why, a fox got me he said and then he ran on until a man stoped him so you no who was calling for help Yes I was me why the man a fox got me the little boy said then he ran on he got him but befor he got in a lady and a man said come with me so he went until he came to a man said to him did you get got by a fox Yes have you got to parents no we must get you some! what ones do you want this man and lady so they had a wonderful party with a nice tae Jely and cac.

Sometimes, however, the roles are reversed.

Once upon a time there were ten little mice. they lived in a hole the hole was in the kitchen of a big red house. they had a mummy and a daddy they all were very happy but there was one thing that worid all of them. It was because they were afraid of the cat and that one day they might get caugt. one day mummy and daddy mouse were out when somebody rang the telifone. one of the ten little mice answered it and the other mouse on the other side said yor mother and father are chased by the cat. Goodbye. of went the ten little mice and were Just in time to see the cat chasing Mr and Mrs mouse into a bottle. after trying and trying to get the to mice out went off to get a fishing rod. the ten mice stood on each others shoulders and when they got to the top they hold on to each others tails the big mice climbed out and they all went home and lived happily ever after as for the cat she came back with the fishing rod and found no more. The End.

Here the method used by marauding cat and rescuing mice has been taken over from a storybook; but note the ways of referring to the parent mice available to the child author; mummy and daddy, mother and father, the big mice, just as in the previous story the lady and the man could become the 'to Parents'.

The following stage, at seven, shows the way the shadowy figures of 'the little boy' and 'a man', 'a lady' become named, particularized, individualized, as Cyrus the whale, Rex the dog, and Mrs Brown, mother; and the action of the story is not so much an end in itself, as a situation in which feelings about that situation can be named and described.

Once there was a whale called Cyrus. He was only a baby whale and he was not very sensible. One day Cyrus decided that he was very tired of his home and that he was old enough to see the sea, so when his Mother was not looking he swam away. Soon he saw a fish. I'm hungry he said to himself, so he swam after that fish, but it was soon out of sight, by that time he was beginning to want his Mother. He looked round but he did not know his way home! I wish I had not run away he said to himself. He swam a little way to try and find his way home. But the only thing he did was find a fish. Please do not eat me said the fish in a tiny little voice. All right said Cyrus but would you please tell me how to get to my house? turn to the right strait on first corner left and your there, said the fish in his tiny voice. Thank you said Siroos and off he swam, soon he saw his house in the distance. Hallo he called to his mother. Hallo called his mother. So Cyrus got home after all. The End.

Once there was a little black dog called Rex. The people who looked after Rex were called Mr and Mrs Smith. Mr and Mrs Smith were not at all kind to Rex. He had nothing to eat and was very thin. He had to go out for walks himself and find his own food. One day Rex decided to run away he wandered for a long time and that night he tried to find a house to live in. He walked up the path of a house. Bow-wow-wow! he said A lady came to the door of the house and shouted: get away! You don't belong to this house! And she chased him away. Wherever Rex went he could not find a home. He had to sleep on the ground, and it was very hard. But meanwhile back at his house Mr and Mrs Smith has mist him. Mr Smith was sitting in the armchair smoking a pipe, and he said that it was not very nice without a dog running round his feet (although he never let Rex do that). And Mrs Smith said that if Rex would come back they would be very kind to him. Rex woke up that morning, and he thought: I will go home. So he set off over hill and along a field till he got home. He wondered if Mr and Mrs smith would be kind to him but he went up to the door, and barked Bow-wow-wow-wow. And he barked so loud that Mr and Mrs Smith came out. And after that they looked after Rex properly. The End.

Mrs Brown had ten children. She had one husband who worked in a sweet shop. The ten children were very naughty. One day Mr Brown died, and Mrs Brown was very sad. So were the children. They buried him. A few day later Mrs Brown was going out shopping. So she said to the children: I am going out to the shops I shall be away two hours. You be good children while I am away. Goodbye. She went out of the house. Away she went on the bus to do her shopping. What shall we play asked one child. Lets look at books said another. So they went into the room where the books were kept. Look here is a box of matches, said Allan. He took the box and got the matches out. He lit them and dropped them on the carpet. Then they went into another room and looked at some books.'' [the house catches fire, and they send for the fire brigade, which they 'watched with great interest'. Mrs Brown returns, smacks the children and has the house 'mended'.] Mrs Brown and the children lived in it for some days. But soon they began to need a father. But Mrs Brown had a great friend. So she got married to him and they all lived happily ever after. The End.

As well as the correct division into sentences, the sometimes sophisticated use of punctuation, the control of sentence structure and widening vocabulary, this girl is exploring ever-widening aspects of 'what would happen if . . .?' and 'What would it feel like to be . . .?' At the time she wrote, she had no personal experience of keeping a dog, or of a death in the family; she was not coming to terms with what had been but that which might happen, the world of thoughts, feelings, intentions, fears and desires as well as real or fantasy action.

Still at the age of seven, the same child takes up the 'adventure' theme in a new way. Co-operative effort, with two boys as central characters, an explicit statement of the desire for adventure, increased awareness of other people's point of view (their parents' feelings are clearly stated), characterization of the 'Baddies' (who are portrayed as ignorant and lazy through conversational interchanges). The objectiveness of her viewpoint (as Piaget would say, she has the ability to 'decentre') is exemplified in her own correct spelling of 'adventure', and its deliberate mis-spelling as 'adventu' in the note that Jeremy leaves for his parents. Awareness of the relative appearance of time – ten minutes can seem 'about two hours' when you are waiting – shows how the gap between appearance and reality can be dealt with by the use of language. The three stories previously quoted formed part of a book she had entitled *Story Time*. This new story provides the title for a book, in which stories and puzzles vary considerably in length and subject matter to allow for a varied level of reader ability and taste. The title and subtitle show the deliberateness of the intention.

Jeremy and David's adventure
and other little stories and puzzles for little children
By . . . .
Sewed by Mrs . . . . .
A story and puzzle book
Little childrens books series

Like any other good children's book, it is copiously illustrated. The device of chapters has been adopted with an understanding of its purpose. It is quoted in full because it is only in a piece of some length that insights into children's ability to handle (or occasionally fail to handle) a variety of grammatical structures can be seen. 'So', 'while', 'because', 'although', can be met with in children's conversation, but there is less everyday opportunity, perhaps, for use of tenses, such as: 'They had not had very much sleep and they were tired', or 'It was autumn now', which have to be used in recounting something to someone.

Chapter 1: Jeremy's and David's Adventure

Once there was a little boy called Jeremy. One day, he thought I want to have a great adventure somewhere. I will run away. So, he made some sandwiches, and put some water in a flask. He got his Mummy's bag and wrote a letter to his mother and father saying:

'Dear Mother and Father
I have gone away to have a great adventu
I hope you have a nice time
Love from Jeremy.'

Then he crept out of the house, carrying his bundle over his shoulder and whistled a merry tune as he went along.

Soon he saw another boy, who was humming a tune. Hallo, said the boy I'm David. Who are you? I'm Jeremy said Jeremy. Would you like to come with me, on a great adventure? I'm doing some shopping for my Mummy, but I will leave a note and come back. you wait there. Goodbye. Jeremy sat waiting for about ten minutes (although it seemed about two hours). At last he saw David, and ran towards him.. Hallo! he called. And they both set off for their great adventure.

Chapter 2: Back home

Back at home, his mother read the note. Just then, as it was quite late Jeremy's father came home. Oh, Dear, said Jeremy's father. It would spoil Jeremy's adventure if we went after him. So we will stay. So they did.

Back at David's home, David's mother and father read the note. Oh dear said David's mother. It would be a shame to go after him and spoil his adventure. We will stay here. And so both families lived. But they sometimes remembered their children, and wished they would come back.

Chapter 3: Fire!

David and Jeremy walked on. Soon it began to get dark. Lets sleep under that tree. They sat down, and Jeremy opened his bag. He took some of the sandwiches out, and the water. Then they had their supper. Then they said goodnight, and fell fast asleep. When they woke up in the morning, they ate their breakfast. While they were eating, they talked about where they would go next. Suddenly, they heard, help! fire! help! help! FIRE! save me! help, help! help! HELP! fire save me, help, help! save me! FIRE! quickly Jeremy and David dashed up the hill. They dashed straight into the fire and pulled the frightened lady out. My poor pets are in the fire! screamed the lady. A dog and a cat! Jeremy dashed into the fire again, and pulled out a dog and a cat. But the fire was very bad. See that old bucket? asked Jeremy. And see that river? fill the bucket with water, and try to put some of the fire out. I will go and get the fire engine. He dashed off to his own village. He dialled 999 and soon the fire engine came along. It put out the fire, and drove away. Then the lady gave them a pound note each, and thanked them for saving her. Then they said goodbye, and Jeremy and David went on their way, saying: I wonder what adventures we will have next?

Chapter 4: The Sea

David and Jeremy went on, travelling, every day. So that all their food was used up, and they had to find things to eat, or to spend their money. One day they saw something sparkling ahead of them. They realized at once they were on a cliff by the sea. They had some money left, so David said, lets buy something to eat. We haven't had anything to eat since yesterday breakfast time, and then we only had a crust of bread. So they went off to the village by the sea. They bought some fish and chips that were allready cooked and sat eating them on the beach. Yum yum thought David, this is the best meal we've had for a long time. Lots of people were on the beach. When they had both finished, they both looked about the beach. Lets play on those rocks, said David. They went over to the rocks. Suddenly David fell head first into a hole. Jeremy fell in after him. Clink! clink! what was that?

Chapter 5: Captured!
David and Jeremy picked themselves up. Then they heard some more clinking. It sounded very faintly. Then they heard, very, very faintly so that they could hardly hear it, thet in airp! they did not know that it really was, theres someone in here! They also did not no that they had not heard the wisper properly, because, it was so far off. They hung around, very fritened, until they heard a few noises. They turned to run, but there was a rock they tripped over, and fell. Just at that moment they were pulled down a hole again. Then into a cave and yet another cave, then into another cave, were some smugglers were. The smugglers put Jeremy and David into a corner of the cave. That clinking noise we heard must have been money or something that these smugglers smuggled in. Whispered Jeremy. Yes whispered back David. If we had tried to find our way throughere we would have been lost because there was two other holes and three caves. And we would not go the right way. Four caves you mean said Jeremy. It began to get dark and they fell asleep. In the morning they woke up. They had not had very much sleep and they were tired. Bring the boat up you, said one of the smugglers. We will start today. Oh dear, said Jeremy to David, we may have to go to another country. The smugglers pushed David and Jeremy into the boat. Get into the boat said another smuggler. The boat sailed out to sea. They sailed on and on till 12 o'clock in the afternoon. David and Jeremy were fritened and curious. Where were they going, and what would the smugglers do with them?

Chapter 6: The Storm
Suddenly the sky began to grow dark. The sea began to get very rough, and the little rowing boat went Up and down, up and down. The wind was blowing and it began to rain. All the smugglers and Jeremy and David were wet and cold. The boat was washed on and on. The storm grew worse and worse. The storm is getting worse and worse, said one smuggler. Its the baddest storm we've been in said

another. We might be drowned or washed away. said another. Which would be a good job if it happened to you said David. You mean it would be a good thing if it happened to you! roared the fourth smuggler. You dare say that about me! the boats going to france but the storm's washing the boat back to England shouted a smuggler. Both smugglers that were rowing tried to get it going the right way. But the storm pulled the oars and it was very hard to row At the last moment the smugglers could not hang on to the oars any longer. The oars were pulled out of their hands! help! cried one smuggler. help cried another. But the storm washed the boat the way to France.. The storms getting badder and badder said a smuggler. You mean worse and worse said Jeremy. I mean what I say said the smuggler. The wind blew, and the rain rained, and the waves were huge, But the storm still washed the boat on to France. At last they saw France in the distance. When they landed Jeremy said, what are you going to do with us? Kill you! said a smuggler.

Chapter 7: Escaped, and the smugglers captured

Oh! goodbye, said Jeremy. We are going! Then he and David jumped ashore, and ran and ran and ran, But all the smugglers jumped out of the boat and ran, and ran and ran, The smugglers could not run as fast as Jeremy and David. They were lazy. Stop! stop! cried one smuggler. Catch them! panted another. Why did you tell them that we were going to kill them, silly? At least the smugglers could run no longer. They sat down panting. Come on said a smuggler. We better go and get back to England before they tell the police about us. We'll use sticks for oars. But we better have a sleep 'fore we go. So all the smugglers went to sleep.

Now, David and Jeremy had been hiding near by, and had heard all that the smugglers had said. quietly Jeremy and David whispered together until they had thought of a good idea. Then they pulled the boat behind the rock that they had been hiding behind. When they had done that they covered the boat with sand and pebbles and stones. And as the boat was upside down it looked like some sand and pebbles on a rock. Then they dashed off to the houses near by. It was autumn now. It had been the first day of autumn when Jeremy and David had first fallen into the smugglers hole. The houses were all whitewashed. And the pavement was made of cobbles. Then they saw a policeman. Look, said David. That is the policeman that we see around our village. He can speak english. Oh, said Jeremy Lets have a sleep first. And as it had been a long afternoon, with many exciting things in it, the storm, the losing oars, smugglers saying, Kill you! escaped, and a big run. Hiding behind the rock and hearing what the smugglers say Pulling the boat away, seeing the Policeman they were tired out, so they went back to the beach and fell fast asleep. It was nine o'clock in the night. When they woke in the morning they were hungry. So they pinched some food from them. Then they went to tell the policeman. There he was then Jeremy and David told there story to the policeman. So the policeman went to ring the police station. Then he went back to the smugglers and took them off to prison. Jeremy and David watched. They laughed when the smugglers who were still asleep woke up with a surprise. I will get you back to your house! said the policeman.

Chapter 8: Home
So he sent them on a ship home. At last, when they got back to their own contry they went off to their own homes. It took them two days to get there, as it was a long way. Once they went the wrong way, but as they did not know they went a shorter cut. At last they saw there own houses, said goodbye, and went into their homes. There Mothers and Fathers were very pleased to see them. Sometimes they play with each other, but they never ran away again. The End.

A comparison of this story of the six and a half-year-old boy's story of the pirates springs to mind. It would be easy, but perilous, to assume that the difference in treatment of a basically similar plot arises only from differences in background and/or abilities. While these undoubtedly exist, more cogent reasons probably concern such factors as the changes in the sheer physical effort of muscular control needed for writing at six, and the ease which greater age and practice give at seven; the different purposes for which the stories were written, which lead to the expression of different attitudes; and the development from imagery used to portray experience as the story unrolls in picture strip form at six, and the incorporation of concepts won from experience at seven — the fish and chip meal bought 'allready cooked', the knowledge that other languages are spoken in other countries, requiring the device of the known policeman, who spoke English: the general development to the 'concrete-operational' stage.

To write in this way at seven indicates the child enjoys using language to explore the possibilities of life. It reminds us that exploration points the way to further growth; this requires the teacher's adaptation to the inner concerns of the child. Perhaps the facilitating effect of non-direction referred to by Nelson lies in the fact that the most helpful mothers were making efforts to observe and understand their children's level, adapt their behaviour to the child's needs. Perhaps they were more able to do this because they were themselves less anxious, more positive in their attitudes to other people.

These 'perhapses' lead on to many other 'perhapses'. Speculation can only indicate how many sided is the problem of socialization, and how infinitely more complex it becomes when interacting with the process it must serve; the acquisition of social symbolism in the form of language, that will change the baby into a human child.

How this may happen has been worked on by Mead (1934). He describes the aspects of the self which develop through inner debate, considering one's proposed actions as they would appear to an observer, and amending them in the light of what one thinks that observer's likely reactions would be.

A view of language use and socialization which owes something to the how-it-happens ideas of Mead has been put forward by Bernstein (1969, 1970, 1972). It is not always easy to be clear, from Bernstein's writings, precisely what is his meaning. He does emphasize (1970) that he is concerned with social organization and settings which he considers determine the types of speech — not the inherent language ability — most frequently chosen to be used. He does not consider the forms of speech he describes as restricted or elaborated 'codes', or as 'variants', which is a later term used to replace 'codes', to be the only 'symbolic order' involved in socializing the child. But he does see these 'codes' as resulting from the way that a class system of society works, and the types of family organization which follow from this. He cautions that social groups today are by no means homogeneous and that the division between elaborate and restricted code is too simple (p 173). He makes the point that speech variants are not 'final and irrevocable'.

The term 'variant' is used to mean the 'contextual constraints on grammatical-lexical choices'. I hope to clarify what is meant by this as I go on. The working-class child is said to make more use of 'restricted' code choices, though he has access to 'elaborated' forms. He is said to be able to express 'universalistic' meanings, i.e. utterances which have the meaning made explicit without the need for any help from context. He is said to be able to use such terms as 'because'. It is social factors which are said to result in him making lesser use of these than the middle-class child. Bernstein argues that it is the role-relationship of *consensus* rather than *difference* which appeals to the working-class child; it is because the use of 'elaborated' speech styles implies the unmanageable role-relationships, the unwanted 'universalistic' instead of the particular meanings the child is orientated to, that he mostly chooses the implicit meanings described as 'restricted'. This is the core of Bernstein's 'argument'. He does not, now or in earlier formulations, say that the working-class child does not possess in his 'competence' the same basic rules of language which are available to middle-class (and I assume, upper-class) persons. What he does say is that *some* middle-class mothers place greater emphasis than *some* working-class mothers on language use for:

... socializing the child into the moral order, in disciplining the child, and in the communication and recognition of feeling ... This does not mean that working-class mothers are non-verbal, only that they differ from the middle-class mothers in the *contexts* which evoke universalistic meanings. They are *not* linguistically deprived, neither are their children. (1972 p 145)

Bernstein is using the term socialization to refer to the process whereby a child acquires a specific cultural identity, and to describe his responses to such an identity (p 162). The complex process of making the child aware of his setting, of what he should do when, and how, is carried out within the family, the peer group, school work. Bernstein discusses the way that class structures give different access to the store of knowledge within society, by ranking the assumed worth of sections of the people. He refers to three components: differences in access to knowledge, the sense of what is possible, and 'invidious insulation', as the components are thought to affect the way that sections of people go about the job of inducting their children into society. Bernstein considers four inter-connected contexts in which this takes place:

1 The regulative context – authority relationships where the child learns 'rules of the moral order', and how they are backed up.

2 The instructional – the child learns about objects and persons, acquires skills.

3 Imaginative or innovative – experimenting, forming his own view of the world.

4 Interpersonal – becoming aware of feelings, one's own and other people's.

How might this be accomplished through speech variants which are the expression of the codes learnt in the family setting? Bernstein makes it clear that he does not refer to people's ability to use fully the rule system of their own language. It is the social rules which he thinks determine use – speech – in particular circumstances, and it is the social rules with which he is concerned:

... the code which the linguist invents to explain the formal properties of the grammar is capable of generating any number of speech codes, and there is no reason for believing that any one language code is better than another in this respect. On this argument, language is a set of rules to which all speech codes must comply, but which speech codes are realized is a function of the culture acting through social relationships in specific contexts. (1970 p 161)

Bernstein qualifies his argument that the speech form follows as a consequence of social relations, by pointing out that the speech form arrived at may itself modify or even change the social structure from which it evolved. Bernstein, as we have seen, distinguishes between 'universalistic' meanings and 'particularistic' meanings, the first context-free, the second context-tied. Those speech codes known as 'elaborated', are said to orient their users towards 'universalistic' meanings, 'restricted' code users are said to be sensitized to 'particularistic' meanings. It is this part of Bernstein's work which has led to wholesale confusions and false assumptions, when it has been used to justify teachers' low expectations of the school performance of the 'working-class' child. The examples which Bernstein gives are of the stories made up by middle- and working-class five-year-old children, or 'constructed' by Hawkins. These are said to illustrate middle-class use of explicit, and working-class use of implicit meanings. Another is of Turner's finding that working-class five-year-olds used fewer 'expressions of uncertainty', that middle-class five-year-olds had more initial difficulty in role-playing, needing a very precise instruction before they would hypothesize about a particular event in a picture. That the stories that working-class children told were 'freer, longer, more imaginative' than the stories told by the middle-class children who were dominated by the form of the story rather than concerned with its content.

Bernstein gives examples, which are composited from noting a number of children's story-telling around a sequence of pictures. These are said to show how the working-class child leaves the meaning of what he is saying implicit, by using pronouns to describe participants in the action.

This explanation of his 'concrete' attitude can of course be construed in several different ways. The use of pronouns such as 'he' could be argued to show greater familiarity and ease with normal language use than the stiff 'the boy'. Another interpretation could be in the working-class child's greater familiarity with a number of adults from an early age, which leads him to be less shy and anxious with strange adults than the relatively more sheltered middle-class child. He could therefore be more intimate in his style of address, assuming shared contexts as intimates of any class do. This, however, is speculation and cannot be more, since the stories describing pictures quoted by Bernstein are hypothetical constructs, not actual examples of children's story-telling or writing.

Study of children's writing shows that they do not write at one particular level, style, or length. Wide variations occur within very short periods of time, possibly because of differing moods and *purposes*. One should never forget that the child writes for a purpose, and often this is to discover things about himself and others – what would he do in a supposed situation, what would others do, what would happen if? So a large part of children's story writing concerns events in real or imagined families. They may also recount stories they have been told, or read, incorporate their dreams into story form, write stories-within-stories in Arabian Nights style, incorporate elements from life, from stories, from T.V., express their ideas of good and evil, life and death. In the early stages of writing, they will seek to replace the emphasis and intonation of spoken language by repetition, use of large writing or capitals, supply their own feedback by confirmatory phrases. They may slip as easily into the framework of the cumulative story, the comic strip, the story-poem, the device of chapters. It is all grist to their mill; the felt need of the moment, to be completed or abandoned half-way according to the continuation or solution of the problem which concerns them. To narrow down, as in the Bernstein example, any assessment of a child's language ability to the ability to tell a story from one set of pictures, is to overlook both the child's need for purposefulness, and the unnaturalness of the test situation.

This should not be taken to mean that it is not a valuable experience to listen to what children have to say about a series of pictures. Gulliford (1971) for example, quotes two very different reactions when John and James describe a picture of a house on fire. Several of the possibilities for the inferior language use of one child are suggested, and the hampering educational effects sketched that will ensue for this child – if the sample of his language is typical (p 166–170). The cautionary note in the last phrase is salutary.

For even within one family, children's story telling can show startling changes. In the story of the bear cubs, at seven years one month, a child again takes up the theme of family relationships, and 'what would happen if . . . ?' Ostensibly he is concerned with what would happen to the bear cubs, but he is also rehearsing methods of tackling like problems should they occur. Feelings and motives are now taken into account. The story ends suddenly when its problem situation ceases to be relevant to the author. The story which follows it, 'The Prehistoric Monster Bird', written by his sister at nine years two months, also grapples with the rhythms of life and death, good and evil. It shows the influence of myth, T.V., and story, assimilated to the process of mastering reality through imagining.

Chapter 1: The Bear Cub

Once upon a time there lived a bear. it was a lady bear. And she wanted some children but she had not got any. On Day She saw a man bear. She said to him Will you be my husband, yes said the man bear I will be your husband. So the man bear and the lady Bear got married. The lady bear stopped the man bear once. and she said to him dont you think that we should go up to the mountains and find a home and have children. would you think that would be nicer. said the lady Bear. Yes said the man Bear it would be much nicer than staying here so lets go up to the mountains and find a home there and have children it will be just very lovely indeed. So off went the lady Bear and the man Bear to the mountains to find a home and have some children they went very slowly then they ran very very fast because they had seen a very lovely home and they did not want any other animal to get it. if it did thow they would scare it out at once then they would settle down them selfs. But no other animal did get there before them so they went in the father went away hunting soon so the mother was alone. She stopped in her home for two months waiting for the Babies to be born. Soon the baby Bears were born and playing but still the father did not come back, the mother Bear did not worry because she was looking after her cubs. there were two of them one was a boy Bear and the other Bear a girl. they were both very nice. the boy Bear was dark Brown and the girl Bear was a yellowy colour they were both lovely Grizzly Bears when they were both two weeks old there mother told them that they must stop there play and come out into the world for the first time. She said it like this come come stop your play and come with me the cubs had already learned to do what there mother tells them so they stopped there play and came with her off they went along the mountain soon the cubs mother said to the cubs now we will have to go back to our own house so off they went very quickly hom on the way home it started to rain. the cubs mother made an umbrella for them [using her body as a shelter. The method was 'lifted' from a story-book.] When they reached home the cubs were safe and sound and dry.

Chapter 2: The cubs mother ill
One day the cubs were playing in there den when there came a banging noise and a roar then it was silent again. the cubs mother rushed outside and found her husband lying dead. then she looked at him and went away the mother Bear was very very sad. it was spring and there are lovely flowers the cubs brought her some of them to eat. She said thank you and she ate them. That did not make here much happier it only made a very little difference Then the mother Bear got up and went out of the den. into the fresh air and ate some flowers and leaves they were lovely they realy were lovely. then the cubs went out of the din and ate some flowers and some leaves the same as there mother. It had realy been a very nice day for for the cubs but just one thing had been very very sad because there father had been

shot it was realy very sad indeed. It was getting dark so all three Bears went back into there den when they got in the cubs started playing again but there mother soon stopped them and said you must go to bed now so off you go the cubs did what there mother told them and they were soon fast asleep. the next day when the cubs woke up there mother was still asleep. they went over to her and tried to wake her up but they could only make her groan and that was not very much help was it the cubs were very very sad indeed the mother Bear was ill the cubs were realy very very very very very sad.

Chapter 3: the cubs mother dies

One day the mother Bear asked the cubs to go outside and fetch her some flowers and leaves to eat the cubs did not think she could talk but they went and fetched the flowers and leaves Just the same as there mother told them they realy wanted there mother to get better they were realy very willing to do anything realy anything to save there mother from dying. But she was getting worse getting worse all the time the cubs could not do anything to help at all. At last the cubs decided to go down the mountain and see if there was any danger or if there was and is any other animal that will help them and there mother they searched the whole mountain but there was not one single animal that would help them and help there mother it was sad that she was ill it Realy was. Just then the girl Bear said if our mother dies then we will have to look after ourselfs and that would be very nice would it not said the boy Bear But we would have to would we yes said the girl bear we would indeed the boy Bear said that he thought they would have to do it because there mother was getting worse every minute and he said that he thought that soon she would die by now it was getting near midday so the cubs went outside the den and got something to eat when they had a big feast they brought some food in to there mother but she was so ill she could not eat it so the cubs ate it. She was getting so bad that both of the cubs thought that there mother was goin to die Realy they did. Really. Well in a few days the cubs mother died so the cubs were left to look after themselfs without a mother or father alive Really the cubs did not like that home so they went out to look for another one.

Chapter 4: The cubs grow up

Soon the cubs saw a very thick clump of trees they went into it and looked for a home at last they found a lovely one near the middle of the clump. both the boy and girl Bear were tired so they went in and went to sleep it was nice home so they soon found a nice comfy place in the den and were very soon fast asleep they did realy like there new home it was realy lovely it was realy as they thought that it was much much better than the one they were born in and there mother died in it and so did there father they did not like it themselfs either. In the morning they had grown a little but not very much bigger. Now they were realy growing up but they were still cubs. first they did go outside and get something to eat they ate some flowers and some leaves and some cabbages and some mice and the last thing they ate was some ferns they were very thirsty so they drunk some water from a hollow rock then they went for a together along the mountain then when they had gone a long way and went back there den. soon they decided to go outside the den and see if there was any danger if there was not they would have a sleep luckily there was not any danger so they went back into there den and went fast asleep. In about three hours the cubs woke up it was getting near midday and the cubs thought it was too so they went outside the den again to eat something they ate the same as they ate before it was some flowers and some leaves some Grass and a few mice and of course the thing was some lovely juicy fern they were nice. now of course they were thirsty like they were before so they went to the same rock as they drunk before but it was dry so they went off. soon they came to a little stream they thought that it would be a good drinking place so they drunk from it. After that they went back to there den and had a lovely long . . . sleep in there den. They realy were growing up they realy were. In about four hours they woke up it was about five o'clock. so the cubs got up and went right out of the den went out of the clump of trees went down to the stream that they drank from before and had some tea. They had some flowers and some ferns. Of course they were thirsty so went to the stream to drink a drink there. After they went back into the den again and went to sleep again. for the night. In the morning the cubs got up and looked around the cave got up and looked around them again the cubs realy realy truly were growing up.

Chapter 5: The great fire
They went out of the cave and sniffed about the air, they could smell something they looked very hard and saw —

. . . .

a very very very very very very big huge fire burning the whole forest. All the animals were running about terrified luckely it was burning fast toward a huge river the part that reached if first soon got out but not very good it was partly going the opposite way from the river and that was making it spread so it was making the fire stay the same size as before but then it stopped spreading and slowly shrunk down to a small fire and then it was gone. all the animals were telifed they all went to the river had a drink went back to their homes or dens and went to sleep for a very very very very very very very long — time for three days. and then woke up.

Chapter 6: Rain rain rain for the animals

Suddenly the bears heard a noise they looked out of the cave and saw it pouting of rain it was rain rain rain rain rain all the time just all the time it looked as it could never stop never the revers were flouding in a few weeks they live a very very long way from any river or stream but in a few months the water was in the clump of trees and near there den because if was still raining and it had not stopped once they were in trouble realy realy they were. One day they had to have a very long swim but soon the sun came out and it stopped raining and the sun quite soon dried the water level low enough for them to stand in.

Chapter 7: Bang Bang

When the water was all gone which was in a few weeks there came a Banging Bang sound and a great big howl from an animal and round the bushes crept a man with a gun he shot at the bears but he missed them he ran away again but so did the bears and animals by now the bears were about grown up and were very fierce but kind to young things. And in a few more days there came another sound like the other sound they herd before it was the same Banging Bang noise as they herd before. In one whole month which seemed quite a' long time to them some small stones started to fall from the top of the mountain soon they got bigger than ever so they were rocks they came crashing down onto the Bears house did fall down so the Bears had to come out of the rekege walk round the mountain and find a new home.

Chapter 8: The Bears new home

Soon the Bears found a cave in the side of a cliff with some trees round it. They went up to it looked inside it and then went to sleep on some hay inside if for a very very very very long time . . . And in a few days time they woke up and the boy bear which was now a man Bear said to his sister shall we seperate ourselfs now. Yes said the lady Bear I think we should. So the lady Bear went off to find a new home and the man Bear stopped in his new home he found that day.

You will hear more about the lady bear in another chapter but now let's get on with the next chapter.

Chapter 9: The great hole

When the lady bear had gone out of site came a noise like an Engin of a lorry on the mountain.

But here the story stops. Now it is the turn of the nine-year-old girl. It provides an opportunity to note the development of her style since the story of 'Jeremy and David' written at seven.

THE PREHISTORIC MONSTER BIRD

Chapter 1: A baby

Once upon a time, thousands of years ago, there was a high hill.
And it was called — KINGS CROWN. This hill was in a far-away land,
where there were Gods and Godesses. And at the top of the hill there
was a landslide. If you had the power of a God then you would fly
high above this landslide and enter a crack in the rocks on the very
top of the hill. You would follow the narrow passage until it came out
again into a magic world called Batar. Who was king over Batar? A
prehistoric monster, with his queen. The king was called Dartar, and
queens name was Matar. One day they had a little baby monster and
they called him Hartar. Now Hartar will tell you his life story.

I was in an egg. A yellow egg. I was a little baby monster bird. I
was about two inches tall, and six inches long. I was wet and yellow
with a bit of brown on the head and a touch of purple on the end of
my tail. I ate away the egg and tapped at the shell. I came out wet and
draggled. Soon I was wriggling on the ground. Then I looked up and
saw the faces of my parents. Matar nudged me with her wet beak,
and I looked up into her gentle brown eyes and loved her at once.
Then I felt strength coming into me and I tried to move. But I was not
strong enough yet. I was pushed down again.

A few days later I looked around me. I was in a cosy nest in a tree,
I was on top of a hill with a meadow and a stream running through.
Actually I was still on Kings Crown. The side I was on was the magic
side. When I grew up I was to be King and rule over Batar. But I had
a hard life to go through. There were wicked creatures who planned
against me.

My mother and father brought me food all day. I grew so huge that
I could not fit in the nest in a few weeks. Then I learned to walk,
sing, croak, swim, dive, fly, to get food for myself and look after
myself. That took me a whole year. I was born in spring. In summer it
was warm and beautiful. In Autumn the lovely fresh mornings were
cold but nice. In winter it was really cold. But I grew strong enough
to stand it.

Chapter 2: When I grow big

It was Spring again, I was now 50 feet long and 20 feet tall. I had
fire flaming from my beak, a grey head matching my two legs. There
was brown along the top of my head and I had a purple on the end
of my tail. The rest of my tail was brown and my body was orange.

Early one beautiful Spring morning I set out to seek my fortune.
Then I hoped to come back to Batar with a princess monster bird and
when Datar died rein over Batar. I flew high over mountains and
valleys, woods, forest, rivers. I flew on for days. Sometimes I landed
to see what I could see but had no luck. One day I came to the

seashore. Quickly I dived down and caught hold of a sea monsters neck. There was a great fright I struggled and bit and fought. The sea monster wriggled and squirmed for he was a snaky blue sort of creature. The fight went in for a long time. At last I killed him. I dragged its body behind some rocks and had a feast.

It was a long flight over the sea. I saw all kinds of sea creatures in my flight, big and small with all kinds of colours in them. One day I came to an island with trees, streams, grass, with pretty flowers growing on it, and hills, valleys and mountains. Here I lived for a time in the middle of a forest. Once when I was out hunting I met another monster twice as big as myself. As I still had my small crown on my head, he at once knew me at the prince of Batar. The monster pounced on me. It was not much good fighting him for he was so big. I was carried off to a huge cave where I was kept prisoner for three years. It was dark and gloomy there. The leader of the island had caught me and kept me prisoner. He did this because he wanted me out of the way while he and his band captured Matar and Datar so that they could be King of Batar. From doing this they could have great power, and perhaps one day rule over the whole world.

But all this was later on. Before that I was sent to the leader (whose name was Rattarfella) who decided to eat me. But then he said 'No, I will not eat him, for when I am king he can be my slave'.

So I was kept prisoner for three years in a cave with guards at the opening. But how did I get to know about Rattarfellas plot against me? This is how: When I was brought to my cave I searched it thourally all for ways of escape. I found nothing but a crack in the walls of the cave, and I covered it up if anybody came in, with rocks. One night when I was tunnelling about a year after I had started I came to another cave. There I met another monster bird rather like me who was also kept prisoner. Her name was Tufty. She told me this:

'One day I was in my cave when I heard Ratafella taking. He said that he captured me to get out of the way so that he could capture Matar and Datar and perhaps one day rule over the whole world.'

Tufty also told me that at the end of three years they would capture Matar and Datar and on that night there must be no-one to guard us, so we would get to Batar first to warn my parents. So the three years past.

Chapter 3: Who will be king?

One night we found that all our guards had gone, and we realised that it was the night they were going to carry out their plot. So we broke out of our cave and soared into the direction of Batar. We flew over the sea, over the rivers and mountains. One night I saw Kings Crown in the distance. If I did not stop Rattarfella in time he might trick the Gods at the great gate of Batar, and march through the land with his band. Quickly we flew to the gates of Batar and arrived the same time as Rattarfella. I called down to the Gods at the gate not to let them through in any way. Then I went to Datar and told him what had happened. So Datar called every living thing in Batar to him, big or small. The army marched to the gates of Batar, led by their leader, Datar. Then there was a great battle. Later it was called the battle of Batar and was very famous. When we were going through Batar some of the great monsters twice as big as ourselves pounced on us and captured some. The ones that could fly did, and the others had to walk. The little ones crept along the ground and tried not to be seen till they pounced. Soon we saw Rattarfella and his monsters. They looked very savage and angry, because Tufty and I had escaped, because we had beaten them to Batar and told Datar, because the Gods would not let them in, because they were cowards and did not want to fight so many millions of monsters (though he had bigger ones himself) and because he did not want to make a fool of himself by flying away, and also now that so many creatures were against him that he probably would not be King of the World. There was a great battle but Ratterfellas monsters or monster birds were so huge that it was very hard for both sides, even though ours had millions. All the time the Gods and Godesses watched the fight. At length, when the fight got very difficult, they joined in. Of course they were on our side, and they helped us by each time one of small monsters was hurt, (not dead) they made them better so they could carry on fighting. The leader of the Gods, Iffa, did not let them do anything else. At length we won. Rattafellas army fled away and was never seen again. There was a great party, with the Gods and Goddesses there too.

Chapter 4: A Happy Time Except for death

At the feast I was married to Tufty, and we were prince and princess. Everyone in the whole of Batar came to the feast, whether they were smaller than a mouse, or ten times an big as an elephant. We had to eat the meat of the dead monsters of Rattarfellas army. At one o'clock in the morning every creature there went away, and that one special night no creature of Batar ate another creature of Batar. For many years I lived with Datar, Matar and Tufty until one day Matar ate a poiseneus plant, and she was very ill for six months and then she died. She was buried on the top of Kings Crown and everything was very sad for a year. The trees had no leaves, nothing grew, and then Datar died of grief. I was now King and Tufty queen, and when they got over the deaths we had a procession and an evening flight to celbrate it. But the next spring we made a nest ready for babys. One of us could only just fit in it to hatch the eggs and keep them warm. One day Tufty laid four eggs. They were yellow egg like the one I was in. One day the eggs went crack, crack, crack. We called the babys these names Baffa Biffa Boffa. We taught them to do many things throughout the year. Soon they were big to fit in the nest and then they learnt to fly walk swim run dive, to look after themselves. In summer it was warm and beautiful, in Autumn it was fresh but cold, in winter they were now strong enough to survive in the cold winter day.

In the spring they set out to find a new home for themselves and we had another lot of babys. Another year passed, and yet another, still another. Each Spring Tufty laid some eggs. Then we did not have any more babys. Ten years, passed peacefully and the end of each year every creature in Batar, and every God and Goddess had a great procession through Batar. At the front were the Gods, then Tufty and I came next. When we had gone through Batar we always had a feast.

Early one morning news came to us that a huge monster had arrived called Ammatar with 42 million monsters as big as big as himself. He had come to fight for King of Batar.

Chapter 5: Another Battle

There was not time for us to do anything else. In came marching these monsters who had taken no notice of the Gods at the gate. They chased every one of us out, drove us out of Batar, far away, miles away. Any creatures they captured they killed. I was chased miles away from anywhere and one day they lost me. I followed a river up and I found a safe island on a lake. Near here I found some more creatures and Tufty was with them. I led them to the island and we lived for five years. In these five years we sent messages to other monsters of Batar that we were here and told them to come to us. So we built up our army to chase out Ammatat and his army. For of course Ammatat was King of Batar now. He changed everything. The Gods and Goddesses had gone. He had even named Batar differently.

So we found more creatures to fight with us.

We got ready for a charge. We took off. When we looked over Batar we saw a great change. I did have a shock. All our beautiful things were gone. I had never seen such a mess. When I gave the signal half of us swooped straight down in to Batar. There was a great confusion as Ammatat did not know we were coming. Ammatat had no time to fight. There had never been such a tremendous fight before. It was called the Battle of Hatar later on. A second or two later the rest of us came swooping down. This was so sudden that it was too much for Ammatat. He fled away to a distant land and did not see us again. We managed to kill off every bad creature we could find in a few months and soon there were no more to be seen. But although we were glad we had won we still were worried about other things. – *Could they?* There was very much mess to be cleared up in a short time for they might make another attack. Could they make the country beautiful again? Would the Gods and Goddesses come back for there was no possible way of sending a message? Would they be safe enough to live in Batar for the rest of their Lives and would everything else? *Could they?*

Chapter 6: All's well that ends well

It was very hard work to clear everything up again but we knew we had to do it. We did clear everything up but it took us six months. We also did it very thoroughly. The Gods came to see what had happened and when they knew that we were back again everything was as it had been before.

I lived in Batar a hundred years. I began to die of old age, and so did Tufty and I called a God and Goddess to us and told them this :– 'We are now getting old and going to die., Will you be King and Queen instead of us? 'Yes' they said 'And when you are buried you will become Gods and live with them and meet Datar and Matar there. The leader of the Gods himself said so'.

And that was what happened. Now I live with:
The Gods, Tufty, Godesses, Matar, Datar.
And that is Hartar, the great king of Batar's story.

It is less easy to pinpoint the class background of these child writers than to spot the books they have read, the stories they have heard, the T.V. they have watched.

Bernstein's examples beg so many questions about the nature of the samples, the differential effect of an apparently similar but fundamentally different eliciting context, and so on, that a great deal of caution has to be shown about drawing firm educational conclusions from such slight evidence, such speculative theorizing. As Labov (1969) has pointed out it is not possible to control the crucial intervening variables of interpretation and motivation (p 200).

Let us see why it would be a major distortion of Bernstein's ideas to use his work as a justification for the continuation of elitism in schools, as a kind of replacement justification of the outworn concept of a fixed limited I.Q., by an action of a fixed and limited language ability.

Bernstein points to advantages and disadvantages inherent in *both* styles. A restricted code, said to be mainly used by working-class speakers,

. . . gives access to a vast potential of meanings, of delicacy, subtlety and diversity of cultural forms, to a unique aesthetic whose basis in condensed symbols (including use of metaphor) may influence the form of the imagining. (1970 p 176)

Its disadvantage is seen in the way differently focussed experience may be disvalued, or seen as irrelevant to what the schools try to do.
Elaborated codes, said to carry the value systems of the middle-classes, are seen as advantageous to the child in school situations, but some children may well develop acute identity problems:

Elaborated codes give access to alternative realities yet they carry the potential of alienation of feeling from thought, of self from other, of private belief from role obligation. (1970 p 176)

Bernstein does not state how he thinks this alienation comes about; perhaps we can divine his meaning a little better from thinking of this in terms of the different functions which language has in fulfilling children's needs as opposed to educational purposes.

The ways that children use language do not have an exact correspondence with adult use. Insights about the nature of language, and of thinking processes, can come from listening to what children say. Take this children's joke:
Qu. 'What is grey and gooey and comes at you from all sides?'
A. 'Stereophonic porridge.'

It shows how elements of old and new experience are combined and re-combined in the hope of gaining a surprise effect. It shows how word-meanings change; strictly speaking 'stereophonic' is more accurately rendered as quadrovisual; but 'we know what it means'.

Patterns of language use can shift and change focus, but for the pre-adolescent child they carry an emotive meaning, pervading the content of what is said with the feelings it arouses in the children. The neutrality of the language used in the school text books, on the other hand, gives little foothold to the child unused to language which has been emptied of consciously used feelings. The purpose of this scientific 'referential' language, which seeks to describe without being either persuasive or incitive, can be hard for the child to discern or even unacceptable. Cazden (1972) gives an example of how language deliberately 'neutralized' had been used to present U.S. actions in Vietnam in a way the American people would accept. She links this with young people's turning away from what seems to them to be fraudulent uses of language, and their rejection of language in favour of other forms of experience.

Since a perceived purpose is necessary for the initiation of actions and thoughts, the passing on of information through text books, encyclopedias, and dictionaries may be made ineffective through its formality. Hotopf (1965) considers the language of instruction as failing in that it regards people solely as information seekers, rather than also information users. His point is applicable to the uses of 'restricted' and 'elaborated' codes. The direct, straight-to-the-point action-linked speech of the lower working-class child — 'I thumped im cos'e thumped my sister', may be more rational than the qualified, verbose intricacy of a child aping adult styles of talk, where the child's speech may be unrelated to what is actually happening in his life. The child who becomes familiar with many styles, a continuity, an ability to mix or change styles at will, will become more sensitive to the feeling which comes through into written words. It comes through as the expression of the writer's attitude to his reader — his tone; the expression of his attitude to what he is writing about — his feeling; and through the expression of his purpose, or intention.

The reader may not consciously analyze these factors, but we all resent the author who 'talks down' to us, or who is inconsiderate to us through the use of technical terms without explanation, or who makes assumptions by including, say, Latin tags without translations. We also get carried away by a genuine enthusiast, who wants to let others in on the pleasurable field of knowledge he has penetrated. It may be through some such mechanisms that attitudes to language use such as Bernstein describes are brought about. Seen from this point of view it is at the stage of secondary socialization that differential school progress linked with different language styles begins to bite, adversely affecting those children who do not possess a full range of language styles.

There are alternatives to the Bernsteinian explanation for the way in which children socialized in families of varying types show alterations in their rate of educational progress, from their babyhood on.

For instance, Collard (1971) has shown that an important factor in continuing or slowing down the child's rate of development may well be the number of children who are looked after by an adult. With young children she studied, the ratio was 1:5 for those living in institutions; with lower-class mothers it was 1:4; for middle-class mothers, 1:3. There was also wider age-spacing in the children of the middle-class mothers. So they would have more time and energy to devote to their children at the time when cognitive development was proceeding at a rapid rate, from birth to four years of age. It would be a reasonable assumption too that professional-class fathers would have more time and energy to devote to their children.

The effect of family size on interactions within the family is looked at by Clausen (1966). He reports Nisbet as suggesting that a low level of interaction between parents and children leads to a deficit in verbal ability. Elder and Bowerman found through a large sample of U.S. children that parents' attitudes correlated with family size, becoming increasingly autocratic as size increased; rules were not explained, there was more frequent use of physical punishment, less use of symbolic rewards. These results were confirmed by Clausen's study, and the important point is made that these functions of family size cut across middle and working class boundaries. Douglas' (1964) findings were similar for British children, and Miller (1971) found that the factors most likely adversely to affect educational opportunity and achievement, occured 'largely independent of social class'. These factors included the acceptance by children of parents' domination of their thought, parents' primitive and autocratic attitudes, overprotection and lack of real interest in the children, as well as a climate of general deprivation. This primitive and autocratic style is remarkably like the picture which Bernstein presents of 'Do as I tell you' as a working-class style determined by language use.

A variety of other factors could also affect the warm mother-child interaction we have seen to be a sign of response to mutual needs. For instance, cross-cultural studies show that the degree of maternal warmth is a function of the degree of privacy available. It varies according to housing conditions. The greatest degree of warmth is shown by mothers who have a median amount of space, being neither overcrowded nor over-isolated.

Care should be taken, then, not to interpret family styles in terms of those forms in which they are most readily discernible. Nor do they operate as a one way system. The two way nature of the process is emphasized in the approach of Speier. Cicourel's analysis of language use is on similar lines, as both he and Speier build on the ideas of G.H. Mead (1934).

Mead saw the basis of meaning as tripartite and reciprocal in form: initiation followed by an adjustive response, resulting in interpretation, the social act. There is a to-and-fro between people, or between a person and another imagined person. The first person speaks, or thinks, but adjusts this to fit the real or imagined response of the other. His speech is the result of this interactional process, through which one comes to know what to say to whom, in which situation. Thus, for Mead, the symbolization of language exists only through the context in which it occurs. Language is important for meaning, since it lifts it into the realm of conscious awareness and in so doing, makes it significant. It provides a form of behaviour through which the person can view himself objectively, by taking on the attitudes which others have towards him, imagine how he appears to other people, then how others judge that appearance; and then himself react to the imagined impressions.
It is where:

. . . he not only hears himself but responds to himself, talks and replies to himself as truly as the other person replies to him, that we have behaviour in which the individuals become objects to themselves. (p 139)

This can be illustrated by a passage from *Jane Eyre*. Jane is brooding on the mystery of Grace Poole's position, and her seeming power over Mr Rochester (with whom Jane, in spite of herself, is by now head over heels in love). She conjectures a past love affair between Mr Rochester and Grace Poole, then continues:

. . . 'No, impossible! my supposition cannot be correct. Yet,' suggested the secret voice which talks to us in our own hearts, '*you* are not beautiful either, and perhaps Mr Rochester approves you: at any rate, you have often felt as if he did, and last night — remember his words: remember his look: remember his voice.'

Indeed, much of the fascination of this novel lies in the way in which inchoate inner monologues, 'the secret voice which talks to us in our own hearts', are made explicit as Jane struggles to resolve experiences which, because she lacks the key to the secret of Thornfield, are bewilderingly inconsistent; and feelings which, because of the tensions between social conventions and her own inner nature, are contradictory. Her dialogues with Mr Rochester also take on some of this quality of reverie, in which our everyday misunderstandings of meaning are absent. It is unconventional talk, intellectually satisfying to both of them; and quite unreal. It stems from one mind only, but holds us spellbound by representing our desire to be able to communicate with some one person without the barrier of inadequate interpretation of the thought behind the word. Vygotsky (1962) gives examples from *Anna Karenina* of people who know each other's thought so well that they can read sentences compressed only to the initial letters of the words used; he discusses the characteristics of inner speech, its compression, and the ways in which it can dispense with outside references.

Another aspect of this talk either to oneself or to an intimate who is almost oneself, is in the use of private language; the carrying over of childhood terms into adult usage; as in the 'Little Language' of Swift's *Journal to Stella*.

The function of this kind of language use in the shaping of the child's idea of himself, reflecting what he thinks others think of him, and how he responds to that estimation, is to enable him to absorb experience through mulling over what has just happened and to imagine what might happen next. It is a major distinction between, for instance, animal communication of warning or mating calls, and human language, that people can reflect on their experience, plan future events. Examples of this kind of thinking abound in the stories children write.

Through the reflective process, Mead continues, two aspects of the self arise. These two parts of ourselves can be regarded as the 'I' and the 'me'. The 'I' is the response made by a person to the attitudes of others. The 'me' is that organized set of attitudes which others posess, and which are integrated into the person's responses. It is that self which we are aware of. Mead cites as illustration of his meaning, the situation in a ball game, where someone throws the ball to another member of the team, because of his awareness that this is the demand being made on him. That describes the 'me' aspect. The success of this response which the player makes, is uncertain; he may throw badly, or he may throw well. But it is that particular response of his, in all its uncertainty, its novelty, which constitutes the 'I' as the response to the 'me' of the organized attitudes of the other players.

Much of this, though not in Mead's terms, is discovered by the child in play, in stories, and in dramatic play which features the child taking on the role of significant others: 'pretending'. Young children act and draw, and later write about, their mothers, fathers, policemen, baddies, doctors, nurses, with an intensity that does not recognize distinctions between reality and pretence. I have seen a child, who, in her real self, was terrified of dogs, approach and pat one of these dangerous animals when she was pretending to be her teacher; then revert to terror when she had returned to being herself. Yet, through experiencing what it is like to be another, children can more clearly know what it is like to be themselves; to know what they possess in common with others (their 'Me-ness'), and what is individual to themselves (their 'I'). The child who is denied sufficient play experience, who does not develop imagery, who cannot imitate the adult world in play, is hampered in thought and feeling, since he cannot readily understand the purpose of adult attitudes and activities, cannot come to terms with his own experiences, wishes, feelings. If he can learn to manage these in play, he can face a return to reality. So this type of play is greatly needed by the emotionally disturbed child, who will have special difficulty in managing the task of appropriate behaviour. Play in words is equally necessary to come to terms with who one is and who one is not, and to define what one's attitude to others consists of.

Two examples of language used for these purposes: the first was sung to an improvised tune by a five-year-old boy who resented a request from his mother that he wash his hands before tea:

Oh, blasted you! Oh wretched you!
I hate you — I hate, I like, I love you.
Sometimes you're horrid
Sometimes you're lovely.
And so — o — ome — times — you're miggling.

The second was written by a six-year-old boy during a school poetry lesson:

I like to play cowboys
I feal like I am a
real one I have
a toy gun and
I put 100 caps
in at once but
I don't wear
a soot but
I ant a cowboy.

Regret is here tempered by the recognition of necessity, feeling acknowledged as separated from reality; words make it so the difference between the two is something which can be assimilated into the child's sense of self. It is the reflective reconciliation of the ever-present gap between what one is and what one would like to be. In this sense, it is 'all done by mirrors', the mirror through which language enables the child to become an object to himself.

5
Symbolism and the sense of identity

With the right sort of experience, the five-year-old child may already be adept at 'reading' a situation; he can make the required response without wasted effort.

I met such a child recently. Holding the hand of another little girl, she came up to me as I prepared my classroom, and stood there with an anticipatory smile, silently watching me. She was waiting for me, as the adult, as the person on their own home ground, to initiate the conversation.

If I had taken her to be a pupil at the school, I would have begun with 'Hello, what's your name?' Responding to features which did not appear to fit her into this category, I amended this to 'Hello, who are you?' The girl replied, 'I'm Mr ———'s daughter'. [She named the deputy-head of the school.] I followed this up by asking, 'Are you here for the morning?' 'Yes, I'm here for the morning, but I'm not staying for dinner.' 'Would you like to come in my class for the morning?' 'Yes.' 'Then go and ask your daddy if that's alright.' Without further remark the two children, still holding hands, ran off to do this.

The child's opening statement of her identity showed that she knew that I was not enquiring her name but her status, and she was able to use an impersonal and objective form of reply, that showed awareness of family relationships; and of her father's position in the school. It also provided the needed information, immediately and concisely. We understood each other. Her next reply showed that she treated my question about her length of stay as a request for information of a kind which teachers rather than other adults require. She saw her presence might affect the dinner numbers. The reason for her coming into the classroom was not at any point explicitly stated, but there was throughout an implied expectation that she would be asked to stay. Having gained her end, further talk was unnecessary, but she retained the support of the child who came in with her.

She had succeeded in creating the desired situation through language, used in a way which skilfully interpreted what was expected of us as participants in a social interchange. Compare this ability with that of Sonia, aged eight, who, though able to converse, express her needs and wishes and so forth, was unaware that her father was classed as a grown-up, or that she herself would grow up to be a woman and not a man. This kind of analysis of what children say can be an important source of information to the teacher about what the children know or need to know. It is not merely a question of what is told to the child, but if he knows what to make of the information, or indeed, if he knows that he is to make any use of it. Byers and Byers (1972) have pointed out how important codes of non-verbal communication are for this purpose, making it possible, they say, for the child to learn how to learn from his teacher; enabling him to follow subtle interconnections; account for tone of voice etc., feel secure in what he has learned, and in its significance. It is a means to 'discover himself in the world of people', as Mr ———'s daughter so clearly had done. It also suggests that since these codes vary considerably from culture to culture – in some countries it may be polite to look people in the eye, in others it may be 'read' as insolence – different cultural codes may pose greater problems for immigrant children than we have previously supposed; there may, as we shall see, be greater difficulties here than those we may assume we will meet with in the area of language development.

Children may quickly develop an awareness of the 'me' expectations of the new country, and this can be indicative of a level of development which would not otherwise be apparent. This was so with Ruby, age six. She had recently arrived with her family from Pakistan, and had learned enough English to converse, with occasional gaps where she hunted for the word or expression she needed. She was telling me some incident in which her mother figured, and in the course of this narration she was about to use the word 'mummy'. She hesitated, then because of the likeness to the equivalent word in her own language, thought I would not be able to understand it; she substituted with an alternative description thus: 'my mu . . . my Pakistani lady she say.'

Her ability to see her mum through my eyes exhibited a form of reciprocity, at a time when a child may still seem egocentric in other aspects of behaviour. Similarly, the five-year-old English girl who stated that she was going to marry her brother when she was grown up. After considering her mother's reply to this, that this was not usually done, she supplied her own reason. This was, that if sisters and brothers got married, their children would not have any uncles or aunties.

Children can learn to express inner concerns through the medium of poetry. The children whose poems I quote were six to seven-year-olds, of 'respectable' working-class parentage. Many had fathers working in semi-skilled or skilled factory jobs, a few fathers were police constables; they included Birmingham children, those of Polish or Irish parentage. They were bright, hard working children. They began with composing group word pictures of their pets in which they used sensory impressions.

His ears prick up
His dark eyes sparkle
His coat feels rough
And curly. He likes to play,
To run with his ball.
My Scottie Dog.

A change begins to come over, in their account of a boy's lost rabbit:

My little pet ran and was never seen
We searched for him but he never came back
He went to the country with the other rabbits.

In the following weeks fantasy themes occur:

I found the bridge to toyland
It led to the forest of toy squirrels,
I showed my passport,
Shook a bearded dwarf by the hand,
Then saw the engine puffing by.

And,

I walked into a wood and I listened
I heard the wolf cry in a queer voice
I heard my foot creak on a branch
I heard a snake rustle through the grass
And an owl hoot in the rain.

This theme was to re-occur many times as the children began to write individually composed poems. Lorraine made the first solo effort:

My Poem
When I am in bed I hear
The rain go pit-a-pat
on the ground
I listened to the little owl
I heard a burglar smasing the
Television I heard him
smas a cup and
sorcer and then a window
But I was only dreaming.

This theme was reiterated. In one, a noise in the kitchen was 'a elephant eating buns'; another boy 'heard rats and mice coming on my bed' in his dream; a girl who 'thought I heard a Dalek talking in the garden', describes her fear, adding 'But I was only dreaming as I am glad.' A man in a yellow hat who was 'Horred', a fox who was going to eat the girl up, a snake in a forest, being in a fight with pirates, two green eyes in the dark 'walking before me', are other fears from their 'friting dreams', which they came to terms with by being able to express and explain to themselves with the consoling formula, 'But I was only dreaming.'

As the poems became more individual, the subject matter became more varied, the style more adventurous. Sometimes the children then wrote their 'poems' in prose story form, but with more vividness and life than their everyday style showed.

in the wood
When I was in the wood I heard a bird sing then I went deeper in [the wood] I heard a shot it was a huntsmen he had a gun he shot a baby bird poor thing.

Or,

There was once a kitten who lived all on its own but it loved having a ball of string.

Or,

One day I heard a snack creeping throw the grass when I was in the gungle it scared me my har started to beate but the native came along and killed it.

Or,

I skip so gentley that no one hears me. But my brother skips like a elephant.

Jimmy wrote a rhyming poem:

Little Bird
Little bird, little bird where are you going. I'm going
to do a little choo on the grass in a pach.
Whot will you do when youve chood the grass
in a little rond pach. I will go back with my
little brown sack. on my back.

Gabrielle, who had dreamed of the Daleks, had evidently seen the film *Zulu*, which was on local release:

In the Wild Jungle
Last night I heard the natives tapping on a drum.
I was so scared I terned to run away.

My heart was beating fast,
The natives and Zolos caught me the beat the
drum again. I tried to run away. But I
had to stay. But I had to stay.

Dragons and monsters are other secret terrors of the night. Derek's
is particularly impressive:

A Monster
One nasty night a horrible monster appears, with taste of people in
his mouth with one pound with his hand he grabbed people and
threw them in his mouth.

Ross writes of his monster:

Look at that monster
Look at the monster.
Look look look look look look.
Help its got me. Help its got me.
Help its got me. Oh yes. oh yes.
its got me. Help.

Pleasures as well as fears are described. Lyn wrote:

On the way to school I heard a bird sing a song to me.
It was a blackbird.
It flew down to my sholder.
And sang a song much much sweeter than before.

Fiona:

I know a little man his name is Tom Timed
If I ask him a favour he gives it to me
I like tom timed I think of him at night
and I think of him at noon.

Helena:

It's True
I once had a cat and It's true
I once had a fish and It's true
I once had a frog and It's true,
But where are they?
I don't know.

Elizabeth produced:

A train on a hill he stopes in the station
then cries bo bo bo bo bo biod and then went down
A train on a hill he fell down a cliff and he
made such a noise that everyone jumped in the air.

A train on the lines he slipes on and on untile he
fell down the clif untile he fell
down the clif.

Jane, who had been a rather silent member of the class, wrote two
poems in two days. First,

The still grass among the trees.
The ripple movements of the lake
The swans glide downward as I wander on
woodpeckers knock on trees
birds chirp away the apple blossom is out
pink white and green as I
wander down stream
crooked brooks and snakes to.
budges sit on my shoulder with yellow
breasts as they peck my hair
the sky is bright blue and the cooko cooko cooko
as the night passes through.

A Poem
The corn is ripe in the cornfields.
The willow leans over the lake. singing trees whir in
the wind, as the old hedgehog feeds his children
the lark sings in the sky.

Dreams, walking in the wood, monsters, birds, animals, magic, lakes
and streams, escape from danger, are common themes wherever
children can talk or write about problems, fears, wishes and hopes.
The following story, for instance, written at nearly seven by the same
boy whose story of 'tresher' and the pirates, has been quoted,
shows an altered mood.

In the Magic Forest
Yesterday I had a dream, I dreamed that I was in forest, a magic
forest, I was walking along in this very dark and creepy forest. I kept
hearing rustling but there wasnt anything there. Once I even thought I
saw a witch and a black cat flying through the air on a broomstick.
While I was walking through this magic and never ending forest I
saw lots of little funny looking elfs and gnomes looking at me, I ran
away as fast as I could and fell into a stream in it there was purple
water. I got out of the stream and found I was quite dry. I looked
back and the stream had disappeared.

The Witch and the giant
While I was walking through the forest I saw a giant kicking a witch,
the giant captured me and took me to his castle, there he put me into
a very big room. I managed to escape from the castle by tunneling

with my spade. Another day I met a wicked witch, she pretended to be nice and took me to her house the next night I escaped through a window. Wile I was walking throught the forest I came to a pool with cats, monkeys, and Kangaroos swimming about in it, I walked past it and suddenly the forest disapeard and there was nothing in sight except a few houses in the distance. The End

Children who fear to communicate with language, for instance those who have suffered severe separation or deprivation experiences, may be willing to confide their thoughts and problems through another symbolic medium, such as drawing. This was so with Yvonne. When she was admitted to school at six, Yvonne was regarded as possibly autistic, and certainly showed many of the symptoms of this syndrome. Her face was expressionless, she avoided one's eye, smelled and touched objects as she put them to bizarre play uses, and, on the few occasions when she repeated an adult's words or phrases, her monotonous flat tone of voice also avoided any expression of feeling. She neither smiled nor cried. She avoided other children.

After a long period in which relationships were gradually built up, occasions arose where Yvonne was willing to try, with individual help, the same kind of activities as the other children. This enabled me to show Yvonne how to hold a pencil and use it purposefully.

Her first wavering attempts showed rapid improvement, and she could soon write her name from memory, and began to draw recognizable though primitive human figures. Her spontaneous language use was also increasing at this time. Then on the first day back at school after a holiday, Yvonne traced some pictures and pinned them up: in the place where I had previously displayed some similar pictures, before taking them down for the holiday. Her next embellishment of

the class room was to trace the picture of a cow, which she added
to a row of pictures of animals I had put up. But her interest in
cows continued, and hundreds of painstaking and exact tracings of
this animal, and many paintings and drawings followed during the
next weeks. As I stood watching Yvonne trace, she asked me 'Miss,
is that the cow's face?' She was pointing to its udder, and, knowing
Yvonne, I took this not to be a straight-forward question, but rather
a sidelong attempt to gain confirmation of something that she thought
or conjectured, but was reluctant to express in outright terms.
Confirmation of my interpretation came after I explained to Yvonne
that that was where the cow fed her babies with milk. Yvonne went
straight to the painting table, producing a strangely human looking
cow (see illustration). Many more explorations in paint and pencil

of this cow-mother were made, including one wearing glasses, and
sometimes including rudimentary human figures in the composition.
During this time Yvonne learned to express her emotions, to smile,
laugh, and, for the first time, we saw the tears of sorrow fall. Not only
did she play more, and differently, talk at times, even name herself as
'I', lose the flat monotony of her speech; she showed a quickness of
understanding that could be startling at times. She evidently desired
to have what she saw as the teacher's powers and rights, and went
through a series of attempts to appropriate these by a kind of

sympathetic magic, through a variety of imitations of my appearance, such as making herself spectacles, and a paper wig. As each of these imitations failed in its object, it was abandoned and replaced by another such symbol. During this time, the series of drawings changed, to a form which at that time I failed to understand.

Only much later, and by chance, did I discover that Yvonne was drawing her mother's wig and the stand it was on.

Another change in the drawings was signalled by one of Yvonne's typically sidelong verbal communications: 'Miss, can I show the eyes?' I went with her to the table where she knew she would find paper and pencils to hand. As I stood beside her, she took my hand, over hers, as in the days when I had guided her in the very first of her drawings. I held it there lightly enough, so that it did not impede her as she skilfully drew two large human eyes, and sketched the face around them. Many 'face' drawings followed. At last, a sophisticated lady in evening gown; Yvonne deliberately added to the fingers on this, lengthening them. Since however stylized their representation had been, her drawings of cows had not shown such extensions to to their legs'I was puzzled by these fingers. I asked, 'Who is the lady, Yvonne?' After a silence she answered in a quiet, clear, very rapid way, 'The lady Yvonne.'

Of course, I took the drawing to mean that Yvonne recognized that

her attempts to gain the teacher's powers by disguising herself were failures, but she was coming to terms with this situation through the statements of her drawings. When she was grown up and her hands were capable of doing whatever she wanted with them, she would have her own way, do what she liked. Her drawings had spanned more than two years of her life, and were outliving their usefulness to her. She became more conforming, adopted standards of conduct modelled on lines more acceptable to adults, and, more importantly, showed that she now had the ability to make relationships with new teachers, relationships of the trusting kind which she had not dared allow herself when she first came to school. Not only had drawings and pretence allowed her to work through her problems, it had helped her to be able to talk, because through her drawings she had learned to accept herself as a person. That this is so is shown by a last reminiscence of Yvonne. At one stage of her copying of me, she had continually repeated everything I said. When this became so inconvenient to me that I needed some way temporarily to stem the flow of parrotted talk, I would say 'My name is Yvonne.' This she could only parody by muttering, for she would not speak her own name, or admit her own identity. Yet some time after the 'Sophisticated lady' drawing, Yvonne approached me, and told me, 'My name is Yvonne . . . ', then, an indescribable smile on her face, walked away. It was perhaps her most direct statement of what she knew I wanted to know. Through symbolism she had found her identity.

6

Language and social identity: sub cultures, social and personal handicap

If we should ask a child to add up, say, six and four, and he decides he has ten, it would be a reasonable assumption on our part that he has some number concepts. We would be using his observable surface behaviour to tell us about an aspect of his level of mental functioning. And the behaviour observed, though very limited, is both relevant and specific so far as a type of school situation is concerned. This is not so with many of the tests administered by educational psychologists as part of the procedures for diagnosing learning disabilities. A certain mystique may well cling to these 'objective' procedures, leaving the teacher at a loss as to how to interpret and apply educationally information which may reach her only in the form of the name of the test followed by a number which supposedly tells her something about the child's 'intelligence'.

Part of the trouble is that tests of this kind, and even the terms 'diagnosis' and 'disability' are, as Cowan (1970) states, metaphors borrowed from medicine, and they locate the source of the trouble in the child himself, regardless of context or circumstances. In order to move on to an on-going evaluation and treatment such as I describe in Chapter 1, we need to know both the general strengths and weaknesses of standardized tests, what sort of items they contain, what the remediation they suggest consists of, and what non-standardized tests and information we can supplement them with.

Information should be obtainable from test situations much more quickly than from informal observation. That is their strength. They have been criticized on the grounds that they cannot avoid the distortions due to measurement errors, the bias of the experimenter, and the fluctuating states of the children taking them. They are of necessity highly selective, and confined to questions which have a demonstrably right answer. Both these qualities pose great difficulties for testing an ability as subtle and complex as that of language.

Cowan considers that 'basic, implicit and often arbitrary value assumptions' (p 56) underly any test's construction and the criteria by which it is validated. It may also restrict the child by 'limiting the range of acceptable strategies he may use in order to demonstrate what he has learned'. (p 56) A test is considered valid if it is in accord with other tests, and its record of present achievement in the form of standardized test scores is often regarded as predictive of both future academic achievement and success in life. In reality, the correlations are low. There are so many other factors to be taken into account. Some of the learning environments of home, school, community, the physical and social surroundings which affect the child, are proposed by Cowan in the following table. (p 55)

TYPES AND AMOUNT OF STIMULATION

Physical	Modes of learning	Social
Stimulus organization	Verbal vs. nonverbal	Number of people in the learning situation
Patterning	New vs. familiar	How others are involved in the
Complexity	Structured vs. unstructured	learning
Intensity	Type and amount of reward	Their attitudes to learning direct
Variation	and/or punishment	teaching
		Provision of opportunities for learning

PLACES

Home, School, Peer Group, Neighbourhood

This partial list of learning environments could usefully be kept in mind or referred to while reading the section which follows. For in attempting to describe language learning as it interacts with social settings and individual reactions to this, the only certainty is that of disagreement. There is much that we just do not know, and the diagnostic and assessment tools to our hand are primitive in form and inadequate in content. Nevertheless, as tools they do enable us to do more with than without them. Our own value judgements are also needed to help us make a conscious choice from the very different viewpoints which I shall describe.

Many children of immigrant parentage have difficulty in learning at school. So do children from low-income families, whether immigrant or not. This has led to the concept of 'disadvantage', and language lack has been put forward to account for the children's difficulties. I am going to consider how the social expectations of child and teacher are involved, presenting a point of view which will surprise the teacher who does not question the notion that immigrant children are linguistically deprived. I suggest it is worthwhile to reconsider. The use of dialect may not be the only reason for the observed difficulties of 'bright' black children in school.

The concept of the 'disadvantaged' child, a great and growing problem in U.S. cities, resulted in a number of pre-school programmes beginning around 1965, which attempted to give children from the poverty-stricken inner city areas experiences which, it was hoped, would give them a better start in school. Methods varied widely. Results can be interpreted even more widely. They need looking at with great caution. Halsey (1972) discusses the various ways 'poverty' has been defined, and in what ways the American experience can be considered comparable with the British experience.

A review of 'pre-school compensatory programmes' by John and Moskovitch (1970) includes a reference to their own programme of 'guided discovery'. They used story based methods of 'verbal interaction' aimed at stimulating the children's communicative competence and expanding their vocabulary. They worked with a small sample of children and their comment is that the programme 'revealed some gains'.

One of the many problems in evaluating such programmes is that each of the 'samples' used varies widely in its own inner composition and in comparison with any other small sample group chosen. This is complicated by the variety of possible ways of interpreting results obtained and further complicated by the wholesale application of firm conclusions from Bernstein's tentative approach to the problem of school failure. The considerable problems of long-term evaluation need further examination, both in the light of the linguist's ways of looking at language performance which we have discussed, and on the sociolinguist's study of language in its social context. As Kochman (1964) puts it:

Given a moment's thought it is quite apparent that most of the world's schoolchildren (rather than our black children alone) are *not* taught to read and write the same language or language variety that they bring with them from their homes and neighbourhoods . . . The learning gap is on both sides of the ghetto wall, rather than on one side or the other. (pp 69, 77)

It has been widely assumed, sometimes from a misinterpretation of what Bernstein said, that language which differs from that used by the main groupings in society must be deficient. Yet Sapir (1963) claimed as a linguist that: 'There is no more striking fact about language than its universality. We know of no people that is not possessed of a fully developed language' (p 93). This is not how Bereiter and Engelmann have considered the language of the pre-school urban child. Their programme had the aim of enabling the 'disadvantaged' child to benefit from school learning. Osborn's (1968) review of the work done provides a useful commentary. It is written from the point of view of a teacher using the programme.

In the Bereiter and Engelmann programme, three teachers each have a group of five children for a $2\frac{1}{2}$ hour day. Language, arithmetic,

107

reading are taught for 20 minute periods. There is a 15 minute break 'for juice' and 1 hour of teacher-directed group activity aimed at consolidating the lessons.

The teacher leads her group in a language pattern of statement, question, response. These 'pattern drills' are based on examples with familiar objects, and the children are taught to reply quickly and rhythmically, in unison. The teacher's praise is related directly to the task, or the child is told 'No you're wrong', and a correction is made, both to the child and in the teacher's method of presentation.

The first task is to learn to replace the labelling of objects with description by a statement. So familiar objects are always used. The identity statement is taught first, always in the form 'This is a ———.' The children are then taught the negative form of this statement, with correction of 'ain't' or a double negative. (This could be linked with the child's difficulty, referred to by Osborn, in making a 'not' statement. The double negative e.g. 'There ain't none' is met with in many dialects.)

In discussing the Bereiter and Engelmann programme. Osborn lists eight language characteristics observed in the four-year-old 'disadvantaged' child. He is said to:

1 Omit articles and other function words. From the examples she gives it is not clear whether this is due to telegraphic style or dialect use. Even if it were 'telegraphese', indicating language delay, it is still indicative of competence.

2 He does not appear to understand the function of 'Not'. Again, the cause is unclear, since it is this type of response which is affected by the child's poor self-concepts, anxiety, and low expectations about himself.

3 Use plurals incorrectly. This can be attributed to his different dialect. Since the child is turning what has been said into a form meaningful to him, it is clear that he has in fact understood and processed the information in a way consonant with his own structures and attitudes. A sense of identity with his own sub-group is intensely important to the young child, and he confirms this by his continuation of the language style of his parents. (West Indian children who could not do the Grammatical Closure Test of I.T.P.A. 'correctly' were able to read – personal communication from Miss J. Smale.)

4 He is said not to use tenses to describe past, present and future. A pointing task is given as a test for this, but this in any case does not sample his expressive use of language. Neither does it fully test structural knowledge, since, as Brown and Fraser have pointed out, inflectional endings are not as basic for competence as structures.

5 He is said not to be able to use pronouns. The inability to use pronouns is also dubious, and open to the same objections as for the use of tenses.

6 A task of choosing between a book or a pencil is said to show that common prepositions are not known. Minuchin comments that ability to deal with 'either–or' statements is based on past experience of making choices, and since poverty allows little choice, the child may well not have had this. It could also be argued that, at this level of poverty, the child might not have seen books or pencils, or know their names. Also the objects might be a source of curiosity to him, so much so that he wanted to handle them both and could not inhibit his handling urges. So the test is remarkably unclear, since the child's action may be variously interpreted according to the standpoint of the observer, as lack of preposition knowledge, lack of experience, lack of names for common objects, or impulsivity, or as a natural stage. (Jones (1972) found that failure to withhold response to 'except' items is shown even by 13–14-year-olds.)

7 Inability to describe actions is another stated feature, which could be attributed to inhibition in the test situation. Labov (1969) gives examples of this.

8 The four-year-old, says Osborn, finds it difficult to learn that a pig is an animal. No indications are given to show if these children have ever seen a pig. Many older children would in any case have difficulty in using such a superordinate word category as animal. Brown (1958) has this to say about the use of superordinates in normal young children.

The young child is likely to say 'car' or 'truck' but not 'vehicle', he will know 'dog' and 'bird' and 'man' but not 'mammal' or 'quadruped'. Where he does use a very abstract term like 'animal' or 'flower', he does not usually possess the full category but only applies the terms to some restricted sub class of the whole. (p 217)

The sentence patterns used throughout the language part of the programme are these:

First Order Statements: This is a –
This is not a –
These are –

Second Order Statements: This – is –
Polar .... This cup is big
This cup is not big
This cup is little
This cup is not little

```
Prepositions ..............This cup is on the table
Colour  ................This cup is white
Pattern  ................This cup is striped
Categories...............This animal is a zebra
                         This building is a house
                         This plant is a tree
Shape....................This cup is round
Made of .................This cup is made of plastic
```

Defining rules are given for class terms e.g. 'If you wear it, it's clothing.'

Next comes the uses of and, or, all, only, some. Then verb tenses, expansions, and personal pronouns. Identifying similarities and differences among objects provides a transition to some problem-solving activity, describing attributes of shapes. An example of the desired dialogue after 'several months' of programme is given:

Teacher: Andy, find a figure that is triangular.

Child: This figure is triangular.

Teacher: What size is it?

Child: This figure is triangular and big.

Teacher: Good. What colour is it?

Child: Green.

Teacher: Can you tell all you know about the figure?

Child: This figure is triangular and big and green.

Teacher: That is good talking.

It depends on your criteria for 'good talking'. The 'disadvantaged' child's difficulty, as seen by Bereiter and Engelmann, is that he cannot deal with a sentence as a sequence of meaningful parts. This hypothesis suggests that when a negro child's version of 'That is a big dog' sounds to a white listener like 'Dabidaw', the child is at the 'holophrase' or giant word stage appropriate to the acquisition of language, the stage of the very young child. But, just as Labov (1969) has shown that black children do not auditorily discriminate vowel or other sounds which are the same in their dialect, e.g. 'pin' and 'pen', our own ability to discriminate what the black child says is limited by our own usage. Fry (in Lyons, 1970, p 43–4) states: 'People . . . learn different phonological systems and develop different patterns of sensitivity to acoustic features of one kind or another.'

Labov's criticisms of 'remedial' programmes

Labov's (1969) examination of Bereiter's data includes the

following criticisms. Where the child's expressions 'They mine', 'Me got juice' are described as language which lacks the means for expressing logical relations, Labov points out that many languages use similar constructions without being called 'illogical'. The children do, at certain times, use the non-contracted full form of these statements, depending on such factors as whether the following word begins with a vowel or a consonant. In other words, the child is using rules; he cannot be described as using merely 'a series of badly connected words' (Bereiter and Engelmann, p 113). The use of 'me' for 'I' is a common immaturity at pre-school age, even when it is not strongly influenced by dialect usage.

The rejection of such answers as 'In the tree' to the question 'Where is the squirrel' is shown to be unjustified. We all answer in this way if we have attended to and understood the nature of the question. By teaching the child to produce the full form of reply – 'The squirrel is in the tree', Labov says they are teaching him, not new language, but production of a slightly different form of the language he has already.

Labov considers that there are six steps in the reasoning leading to this type of 'remedial' programme.

1 The lower-class child's spoken response to the formal situation which he sees as threatening, is used as evidence for lack of verbal capacity.

2 This verbal deficit is said to be a main cause of the child's poor school performance.

3 Middle-class children do better at school, so their way of speaking is seen as needed for learning.

4 Class and ethnic differences in grammatical forms are seen as differences in logical analysis ability.

5 Teaching mimicry of certain speech patterns is seen as teaching logical thinking.

6 Children are said to be thinking logically when they learn these formal patterns. It is predicted they will do better in 'tool' subjects in their later school years. (p 205)

Bereiter and Engelmann exemplify the great degree of divergence possible when interpreting data from the same group of children. The common ground they should all share, that is the belief that the city-dwelling poor child can learn, is overlooked in their advocacy of their own viewpoint, hardened into the currents of opinion. One claims language 'deficit', the other language 'difference'. Interest in the quality of language used by 'disadvantaged' children has led to its detailed descriptions by linguists such as Labov, who are sympathetic towards the black urban child.

Labov (1969) has argued for the high verbal ability of negro children, emphasizing the importance of situation for speech. It is, he says, 'the most powerful determinant of verbal behaviour . . . an adult must enter into the right social relation with a child if he wants to find out what a child can do' (p 191). He believes this is not possible for the white investigator, however sympathetic he may be. Labov has adopted the extreme position of considering the concept of verbal deprivation to be a myth which 'diverts attention from the real defects of our educational system to imaginary defects of the child'. (p 180)

Other commentators are somewhat more cautious. Ervin-Tripp (1971) puts it like this:

The widespread belief that there are class and ethnic group differences in developmental rates, leading to 'verbal deprivation' requiring compensatory linguistic training, seems extremely ill-founded. We simply do not know . . . The little evidence we have suggests no differences.

She quotes Williams as interpreting Bernstein's and Hess and Shipman's findings on the class variation in children's language uses as, for the working class child: 'a kind of playing safe, sticking close to context, since the differences disappear when tasks are interpretative and require elaborated speech.'

Bernstein's work has lent itself to a variety of gloomy conclusions, not all of which are consistent with what Bernstein says. It is necessary to re-emphasize that he does not disagree with the notion of 'competence' in language advanced by Chomsky. Nor does he claim that 'middle-class' elaborated codes cannot be used by 'lower-class' children; nor that elaborated speech is in all circumstances better than the 'restricted' code.

The effects on performance, through the children needing to 'play safe' are not identical with the playing safe reasons of retarded children, but they display similarities. Watson (1972) in discussing the reasons for the lower performance of Negroes, shows not only that the stressful performance-draining environment and their realistically low expectations of success were factors, but also that their unrealistically low rating of their own chances of success had an additional cumulative effect. Labov (1969) describing children who appear to lack language, speaks of an asymmetrical power situation where the child 'defends' himself in what seems to him to be a threatening situation. This can be likened to the effects of experience on slow-learners' attitudes to themselves; so that even though the language programmes I discuss were not aimed at the slow-learning population (though necessarily including some of them; a point I will return to) they are relevant to the language problems we encounter in special schools. Poor and limited use shows one side of the problem; another is the lack of conversational appropriateness. We should be aware that linguistic skills include coming to say the right thing in the right way at the right time and place, as defined by their social group.

'Low-income' dialects are themselves quite varied, according to the conditions on which they arose. Several detailed descriptions of their main features are readily available, for example Menyuk (1971), and Hopper and Naremore (1973). Menyuk shows how the same meanings are expressed in the different forms, saying:

It is evident from the structural differences described that there is no grammatical relationship which can be expressed in one dialect which cannot be expressed in another, although different techniques may be employed to express these relationships. (p 223)

She adds that no evidence has been found that low-income black or white children exhibit greater difficulty in acquiring the language of their community than do white or black middle income children (p 225). Both sequence and rate for early language acquisition is comparable. Later on, differences appear according to the age of the child and the nature of the tasks he is faced with. Certain word association tasks showed that low-income children were superior at an early age, then became less able than the middle-income children, then still later the two groups gave equal performances. Different patterns of difficulty with different tasks at various ages was also found (Menyuk, 1971, p 244). It seems that the notion of all round low language ability which had been put forward to account for the well known fact of lower achievement (by and large) in school situations of children of low-income working class families is inadequate as an explanation. It may be just as inadequate to state, as Hopper and Naremore do, that the answer lies in a change of 'our' attitude towards non-standard speech and non-white people; yet attitudes are important. The proposal for 'cultural diversity and working to make each child comfortable within several usage styles' (p 126) which these authors make, is a desirable goal for all children. The problem is how to achieve this aim.

A detailed review edited by Brottman (1968) reports on and attempts to evaluate compensatory programmes developed and used in the U.S.A. (It includes Osborn's description of the Bereiter and Engelmann material.)

The most 'unstructured' programme of Alpern did not show lasting benefits. Strodtbeck appeared to get somewhat more improvement with the more structured of his two groups; but as Brottman points out, questions of design, uncontrolled variables, differences in interpretations and the considerable variations of child ability within any given population, mean that gains may be more an artefact of the sample than a reflection of the programme's effectiveness.

Gray *et al* (1966) developed a programme which emphasized teaching the socialization skills needed in school, a curriculum to develop cognitive skills; using teachers 'trained in early childhood education', with aides and home visitors, intensive interaction with parents, and 'an ongoing testing program'.

Significant differences between the experimental and the control groups in tests which emphasized language competence were reported after three years. Interestingly, siblings were also found to have benefited.

Weikart's Perry Pre-School Project (in Brottman 1968) also involved other members of the family through home visiting, but his main method was 'verbal bombardment', a constant series of questions and comments by the teacher, not necessarily requiring an answer from the child, but designed to give awareness of various uses of language. Weikart's evaluation of results indicated greater intellectual gains when structured methods are used.

Di Lorenzo and Salter (in Brottman 1968) used several methods in an attempt to find the most effective, but seem mainly to have discovered the least effective, which was the Edison Responsive Environment Machine, or 'talking typewriter', and the not surprising fact that all the children who were given any of the pre-school programmes showed benefits over the children who had not.

Minuchin and Biber (1968) describe their approach to children with multi-problem backgrounds, the children of poverty stricken homes. They consider pre-verbal communication and the development of symbolic play to be necessary stages preceding and supplementing specific language work; these should not be overlooked, for, as they say, deficit may have many roots. Their approach, described by Brottman (1968) as 'unstructured', is in fact highly structured in the sense of the teacher being deeply aware of what she is doing, neither forcing language on the child before relationships are made, nor presenting language in situations which give it little meaning. Language is offered as a problem-solving tool in a situation which has rich emotional meaning for the child. This enables him to differentiate his perception and the expression of his own emotional states.

Extension of experience and symbolic play, deliberate techniques to consolidate language in the context of the child's activities, and the grasping of spontaneous opportunities for this, all aim to give language in a way not easily assessed by the usual tests. The true test is seen to be whether the language can be used by the child.

In one of the examples which illustrate her points, Minuchin remarks that the focussing of attention may be one of the most important aspects of teaching these children.

Some of the uses which Minuchin describes putting language to are comparable with Halliday's seven modes (1970) through which the child satisfies his needs, tells others what to do, interacts with them, defines himself, finds out about the world, imagines, passes on and receives information. It is within this context of recognizing all these needs that I see any specific language programme working.

The Matrix Games devised by Gotkin (1968) are not without an awareness of the subtleties of language, and include provision for imagination through 'fantasy trips'. But his main emphasis is on a programmed instruction approach, using materials which represent logical steps. Games were designed which involved pupil-teacher interaction. Cognitive abilities were developed through classificatory skills. The games require clear speech, the ability to follow complex directions, development of new vocabulary and concepts, being an independent learner in this context by adopting the teacher's role. The need to plan methods of classroom implementation is stressed in an interesting discussion. For instance, the way in which a child should be guided from a wrong response to a correct one without the use of 'no' is dealt with. The games require a fairly high level of language understanding and use to be already established, before a child would be able to participate.

Gotkin's own criticism of his results is that although the children got hold of the language and spoke it correctly, it was not fluent – they did not own it. This might indicate a transitional stage, compared to the tea-party scene in *Pygmalion*, where Eliza over-distinctly enunciates, but the content of what she says is inappropriate.

Stern reports (in Brottman, 1968) a pre-school language project with the objectives of teaching children:

. . . to use standard English both as a tool with which to control their environment more effectively and as a conceptual system with which to process information, perceive relationships and perform logical operations. (p 52)

New instruments of evaluation being developed by her include an auditory discrimination test which avoids the problems of knowledge of the terms 'same' and 'different'. The child is presented with two pictures, one real, one nonsense, and is told: 'This is a table and this is a pable. Put your finger on the pable.'

A hierarchy of difficulty of phonemic contrasts, ranging from 'girl' and 'hujuj' to 'fish' and 'fith' is used. A visual discrimination inventory, of 52 items, tests form constancy, figure-ground discrimination, closure and position-in-space.

A measure of the child's range of sentence complexity is reached through a repetition test, which gives sentences differing in length as well as complexity. They range from 'Dogs bark', to 'If the ground is wet, the children won't be able to play in the park.' An expressive vocabulary inventory aims to sample a variety of parts of speech: progressive verb forms, prepositions, adjectives, adverbs, verbs and nouns.

The battery of pre- and post-tests through which evaluation of the programme is made also includes talking about pictures, encouragement to tell stories about them, responding appropriately to the speech of others, drawing inferences, and solving problems which require verbal mediation. In fact, there seems to be more tests than programme, though this type of testing can also be a learning situation for the child. Stern's own criticism is that they neglect affective variables which have a potent impact on the rate and nature of learning. She refers to the work of Glick in showing that many of the I.Q. gains reported are more of a reflection of the fact that the child has learned to respond better to the teacher's expectations, than of improvement in ability to learn the tasks. She comments that an even more difficult problem lies in evaluating the worth of the stated goals.

Dickie (1968) attempts to compare the Bereiter-Engelmann approach and the Gotkin approach with the 'traditional' or so-called 'unstructured' approach. Difficulties in controlling variables, problems of suitable criterion tests, differences in parental attitudes towards types of programmes cloud the evaluation issue, but an important point for slow learners emerges. The children were divided into 'high-language' and 'low-language' groups. Neither of the two reported experiments showed significant differences overall in gains between 'structured' and 'unstructured' programmes. But the 'low-language' children got greater help in learning labelling than the 'high-language' children did. 'High-language' children gained slightly, though not significantly, more from 'traditional' than from programmed. Dickie comments:

The fact that high-language children were significantly different from the low-language children in several of the comparisons points out that within a given 'disadvantaged' population there is heterogeneity. The pre-school program to be chosen may depend a good deal on what kind of disadvantaged child one is dealing with. (p 73)

I would suggest that the type of disadvantage that many of our children at ESN school have may be similar in kind to that of the children described by Dickie as the 'low-language' group. There is a mounting body of evidence that the cycle of poverty, with poor pre- and post-natal nutrition, can have an adverse effect on mental development. Pasamanick, Knoblock and Lilienfeld (in Hunt 1961) found that deficiencies in maternal diet associated with low income resulted in increased birth difficulties, followed by intellectual retardation in the children. Harrell (in Hunt 1961) followed this up by studying the effect of supplementing the maternal diet. The children at two to four had significantly higher I.Q.s than those in the control group. Garn (1966) has shown that it is not just calorific value that counts for the growing infant, but that a shortage of first-class protein (the most expensive foods) can result in reduced brain growth. In another experiment (in Smith and Dechant 1961) Harrell gave a daily vitamin supplement to a group of orphanage children, who improved over a control group in 15 areas related to intellectual and physical functioning. We do not have any way of showing if it is the educational aspects of the intervention programmes which have helped the U.S. children to make progress, or if their attitudes, motivation and confidence were improved, or if improvements resulted from the food they had at 'snack' times. That the U.S. experience is comparable with that of some British children is shown by the report *From Birth to Seven* (Davie, Butler and Goldstein, 1972), which includes the fact that lower-class children can be 1·7 inches (4 cm) shorter than their middle-class counterparts. I am not aware of evidence directly linking the high proportion of small-sized lower-working-class children in ESN (M) schools with the deficits commonly observed in such areas as short-term memory, but it seems likely that this is the kind of function which could be affected by a combination of nutritional and other adverse environmental factors, and it is these children who are not so likely to learn in an 'unprogrammed' way.

The way that poor nutrition affects the unborn child and continues to affect potential development up to the age of two years, has been evaluated by Lewin (1974). Most of our brain cells are formed early on, in the first months of the mother's pregnancy, but Lewin finds some types of cell that form during the last three months of pregnancy. The formation of these, as well as of the vital connections between cells, is definitely dependent on a certain level of nutrition, a level which needs to be maintained during the first two years of life if the child is not to be adversely affected in a variety of ways. (pp 268–74)

An increasing body of this kind of knowledge should help in the prevention of learning and behaviour difficulties, as should our knowledge of the comparable problems caused when children have been exposed to excessive levels of heavy metals such as lead, the absorption of which, through piped water supplies, car exhaust fumes, or factory pollution, is now considered to be a major hazard for many of our city children.

117

One of the American schemes devised to help children who are thought to be in need of language help, has been used in many nursery schools. It is called the Peabody Language Development Kit, or P.L.D.K.

The Peabody Language Development Kit is a source of ideas for developing spoken language. The manual gives 180 lessons covering a two-year course, as well as 396 cards. The approach is systematic, but allows for teacher-centred activity rather than child-centred activities. The puppet, boy and girl figures who can have their clothes put on, the plastic fruits, and many other bits and pieces, show the side of the programme which is a fairly loose collection of ideas. The repetition of sentence patterns until they have become habitual shows the 'structured' side. Some teachers like it because it helps them to organize their language work, but others find it restrictive, or regard its aesthetics as inadequate and its techniques of questionable value.

The 'action programmes' based on the Plowden Report which espoused a policy of 'positive discrimination', reported by Halsey (1972), tried to intervene in four educational priority areas in such a way as to induce change and set up a 'self-perpetuating innovatory habit' in the local schools. There are the usual difficulties of assessing progress made through using the kit with nursery school children, for while the children all made progress, their teachers were divided in their opinions as to why this should be. Some ascribed it to the use of the P.L.D.K., some to the general stimulation of the school setting.

The need for more appropriate materials led to the development of three projects for use in the E.P.A. action-research. The puppet P. Mooney was replaced by Dr Wotever, the whole scheme being called *Wotever Next*. Twenty-four written stories used a selected vocabulary with the planned introduction of new words. The inclusion of local material was encouraged. It was not possible to evaluate this before the project ended.

In a different approach, the aim was to direct the staff's attention to language producing situations, increasing their awareness of language development. The project team concludes that there were indications that the teacher's behaviour could be altered to give more one-to-one contacts, and that knowledge was gained as to which typical pre-school projects could be used for language work.

The third scheme used was the Blank and Solomon (1968) one-to-one language directed teaching plan which actively involves the children in their learning. Again gains are difficult to evaluate; my own feeling is that this corresponds more to children's needs than Peabody or British versions of it.

Language as a tool, and suggestions for helping the child to make

better use of the language he has, are featured in the Blank and
Solomon programme. While this is not designed to teach language
acquisition, it has useful points for the ESN teacher. It aims to
systematize the teaching of language skills closely bound up with
language ability. Daily individual practice is used, so it also increases
the child's interactional social skills. A 'Socratic dialogue' covers the
following nine areas.

1 Selective attention i.e. comparing objects, making choices.

2 Categories of exclusion e.g. draw something then draw something
different in type.

3 Imagery of future events e.g. 'Where would the doll be if it fell
off the table?'

4 Relevant inner verbalization: the child looks at a picture, says the
name to himself, then names it to the teacher after the picture is
removed.

5 Separation of the word from its referent. The child is given a
command which he must repeat aloud before carrying out the
instruction.

6 Models for cause-and-effect reasoning. What is the weather
like? – Why?' etc.

7 Ability to categorize e.g. giving a doll an imaginery apple, asking
what other food it might eat, and what other foods are not fruit.

8 Awareness of possessing language; the child gives commands to
the teacher.

9 Sustained sequential thinking; 'What would happen if?' followed
by the child carrying out the suggested action, thus experiencing
what was discussed.

A look at remedial programmes could not cover all the schemes
devised, but mention should be made of two approaches to the
severely handicapped child who is without observable language
skills. The scheme worked out by Molloy (1965), a carefully graded
series of lessons aimed at bringing understanding through a
multi-sensory approach, first teaching the ability to listen and
proceeding to a spoken response, is very different from that of
Barnes (1970). Barnes uses 'stick' drawings as a model for the child
to physically imitate, linking this with language through the teacher's
spoken words. I would not wish to categorize either of these as
'better' than the other, but to emphasize that the teacher has to be
flexible enough to make use of their work as and where it is likely
to be effective within the general framework of the ongoing teaching

activities in the class. This applies to all language programmes; there is no one 'best' method to fit all children or to suit all situations.

Mittler (1972) has pointed out that the subnormal child, that is, the child most likely to need the help of specific language work, is at a particular disadvantage compared with the normally learning child, in that he is less skilled in indicating to the teacher that he has failed to understand something said to him. He is lacking in that repertoire of behaviour by which we signal incomprehension; the puzzled look, the frown, the request for repetition or explanation, are not often used by the sub-normal child. His facial expression remains unchanged. It is easy to make the false assumption that he has understood. Mittler stresses the need to teach the child to signal non-understanding.

As teachers, we can also see the other side of this coin, in that our own facial expression, gestures and the situation itself help to make it more difficult for us to be sure that the child understands the language content of our spoken message to him, in situations where he can 'read' these cues even if he does not yet use them expressively. This makes it all the more necessary to have good tools for assessing how much of the spoken message is being 'processed' by linguistic rules.

The Illinois Test of Psycholinguistic Abilities has been developed by Kirk (1968) from Osgood's model of language processes. Its use of the term 'psycholinguistic' can be confusing to teachers, since it is a use which is quite different from the current use of the term in theories based on discontinuity from forms of animal communication. But it began to be applied in the early fifties; at this time interest in linguistic analysis to describe language use co-existed with learning theory of the stimulus-response type, and with information theory. I.T.P.A. is concerned with:

1 Understanding, or 'decoding', in order to get meaning out of the visual or auditory stimuli coming in.

2 Expression, or 'encoding', either by words or gestures.

3 Association, or the internal dealings by which language symbols are related in a meaningful way.

These three abilities, the third, by its nature, unobservable, make up that part of the test which is named as 'psycholinguistic processes'.

Two other major areas of language ability are described; channels of communication and levels of organization. The channels refer to what the child can hear and what he can say through the combinations of sensory-motor functioning. The levels of organization are divided into:

a the representational level, which is concerned with the meaning
and significance of those aspects of language which need the
ability to understand, to think about things, and to speak.

b The automatic level, which is concerned with sequencing and
other skills needed for correct word-endings, such as we use in
plurals, or past and future tenses. These are responses we come to
make in an organized and integrated way without having to
think about them.

These three main dimensions are said to be tested and assessed
(a language score can be derived) through ten subtests and two
supplementary subtests, which were added to the revised I.T.P.A. to
try to remedy weaknesses. All in all, it is hoped to assess 'a given
process at a given level via a given channel' (quoted Mittler 1972
p 112).

The comments made by Mittler contain some interesting points.
He says:

Although the test is open to a number of psychometric criticisms . . .
and can also be faulted for failing to take account of advances in
developmental linguistics . . . it does, nevertheless, provide a useful if
not comprehensive model of language behaviour and allows the
clinician to study constituent aspects of language behaviour and to
draw up a profile of a child's relative assets and deficits so that he
can design a corresponding programme of remedial education. In
other words, it does not stop at mere assessment. (p 113)

The need to be clear about what a child can or cannot do is here
linked with the firm belief that something can be done. Assessment
is not seen as an end in itself, but as a means of finding out what is
needed and then meeting this need.

The I.T.P.A. remediation proposed as a result of giving the sub-tests
does not always appear to be relevant to the performance of the
particular task it is applied to; although it may be a useful activity
for other reasons. For instance, a test from the 'automatic sequential'
level of organization, called 'auditory vocal automatic' or
'grammatical closure', tests the ability to form correct plurals, past
tenses or comparatives, by getting the child to supply the needed
word in sentences such as these:

'Here is an apple. Here are two . .

'This box is big. This box is even . . .

'The thief is stealing a pencil. These are the pencils to be . . .

As we have seen in this type of task, the ability to know and use
rules is involved. At about the three-year-old level it is easily
demonstrated when the child over-applies the rules before he learns
the exceptions to them. Thus 'I seed them', 'two mouses', 'actual
cricket', 'I'm newing the bed'. So one would expect remediation to be

concerned with ways of learning rules and their exceptions. But the suggestions, while they include these, are often for general or parallel activities which do not necessarily transfer to the skill considered to be lacking.

The fact that much of the remediation is not directly applicable to the task should not be seen as entirely disadvantageous. Hunt (1961, 1968) has shown how abilities may arise on the basis of earlier experience which is different in kind, e.g. the ability to sit, crawl, or walk may be related to earlier opportunities to see and hear many things. But the trouble with the I.T.P.A.'s remediation is twofold.

The suggested activities may, in fact, be more difficult, some of them much more so, than the tasks they are supposed to help with. They are developmentally later in level. Even where they are not, and where they do relate to the task in hand, their value is doubtful. It has been shown to be an ineffective method merely to correct a child's speech as in the proposed task of identifying the grammatically correct one out of two sentences. Better returns are obtained with young children by an adult who 'models' i.e. provides examples of the desired forms, than from directly telling a child what ought to be said. Other of the sub-tests, such as 'motor encoding' or 'manual expression', where the child has to show how to use an object, seem to depend on whether the child has previous experience of and knowledge about the articles concerned. This criticism also applies to items in the 'auditory vocal association'.
'A red light says stop. A green light says . . . '
'Rabbits go fast. Turtles go . . . '

Nevertheless the test can help us to draw the teacher's attention to the relevance of classroom activities which help language and other abilities. Many nursery and infant teachers do this kind of thing in the form of group and individual games as part of 'infant method'. Miming common actions, for example, would be done through *Here we go round the Mulberry Bush.* Engel (1968) has collected a number of language motivating experiences, and Karnes (1968) has a book of suggestions based on I.T.P.A., using American material. It is often a salutary experience for the teacher to have to define the purpose underlying the lesson activity she is taking, and the I.T.P.A. based materials could, critically used, stimulate this process.

There are a number of other language tests. A well-known one is the Reynell Developmental Language Scale. This also distinguishes between receptive and expressive language. The child makes a pointing response to pictures and is assessed on free conversation around standard materials. Perhaps its main usefulness is that it can help to pinpoint areas where language development is very uneven.

The Renfrew Language Attainment Scale is mainly used by speech therapists for assessment of children between three and seven years old. It tests articulation levels, has a word finding vocabulary which includes naming parts of the body, etc. Using pictures of common activities, questions are asked to elicit use of tenses, plurals, and simple to complex sentences. The child is also asked to retell a story based on a series of pictures. This is scored by taking into account both the information communicated by the child, and the length of the sentences he uses.

One of the problems involved in language scales is the arbitrary nature of the content they use, and the fixed criteria of the scoring. Criticisms along these lines have been made by Spradlin (in Mittler 1972) who claims that they do not take account of the nature of language skills required in a particular community, or the minimum level of language which is needed for a person's adjustment to his community. Spradlin argues for the definition of goals, for using small language steps which have been inferred from the process of language acquisition, and for using the methods of behaviour modification.

Mittler gives a summary of the principles involved in behaviour modification as applied to language behaviour. A psychologist makes precise observations on a carefully specified piece of behaviour. He might note the time spent on vocalization, its nature, or the time the child spends looking at the examiner, and so on. From this he establishes a baseline. A programme of systematic teaching is instituted which it is hoped will increase the frequency of the desired behaviour or decrease unwanted behaviour. Carefully chosen and well timed reinforcement are needed to get the plan to work.

Yule and Berger (1972) describe a number of investigations into the use of this method with children who don't talk. The principle used, as they point out, is that behaviour can be modified by its consequences. By the systematic variation of the environment, and observation of the effects of this on the child, it is possible to specify those environmental conditions which affect a particular child's behaviour.

It is necessary to find out what reward will be sufficiently important to the child for him to start, and to continue with, what it is he is wanted to do. This reward is only given immediately after the wanted behaviour. Most children respond to praise and approval; but where they do not, material rewards should always be accompanied by reinforcement of a social kind. In time, the approval of the adult will in itself come to be the child's reward for effort.

The technique of 'shaping' behaviour, by moving it in the right direction through a series of very small steps, is used. This includes obtaining the most helpful conditions for getting the process started by choosing the situation carefully. For instance, if a child talks with his immediate family but not at school, it makes sense to start his behaviour modification programme by using the family setting, introducing an adult gradually into the situation.

Yule and Berger do point out, however, that Bandura and Lovitt have shown that with socially responsive children, quicker results can be obtained by telling the child what is wanted from him, by showing him how to do it, and by providing an appropriate model. Nevertheless, reinforcement principles may still be important for the child who has failed to talk. Yule and Berger list five reasons for this.

1 The child's motivation may lag when he realizes he is failing.

2 The family may stop talking to the child because of his lack of response.

3 The abnormal lack of reinforcement in the environment may have been partly to blame for the delay in speaking.

4 The unusual behaviour of the therapist may be needed, because the child is not responding to the usual. This can be the case with the 'autistic' child.

5 Some cases of speech delay may occur in children whose speech is also deviant. It is possible the programme will help with discrimination, attention, and motivation.

The authors give details of Lovaas' technique with autistic children. They make the important point that the principles of behaviour modification are easily taught to parents, and may be helpful in developing socially acceptable behaviour and skills as well as language. It is extremely important to evaluate what progress is being made.

Children assessed as ESN(M) and ESN(S) often show weaknesses in the functioning of their short term memory. Investigations were made by Graham (1968, 1970) into the relationship between short term memory and the ability to repeat, to comprehend, and to produce new sentences of certain types. The language model he bases himself on is the psycholinguistic approach of Chomsky. The sentences he devised were similar to those used by Menyuk in that they varied in structural difficulty, and therefore in the amount of processing which they needed, depending on the transformations needed for their understanding or reproduction. So the test sentences devised could be arranged in a hierarchy of difficulty. Sentences to test comprehension were kept to eight words in length to ensure that the short term memory difficulties referred to did not obscure the child's ability to deal with a complex structure.

The three language tasks are related, with the same basic competence underlying them. Comprehension comes developmentally earlier, since additional skills are needed for expressing oneself in repetition or production. Graham quotes the work of Fraser, Bellugi and Brown, which establishes both the connection and the order-of-difficulty notion for different grammatical structures. If a child could be brought to produce a sentence, it would show that difficulty in either comprehension or repetition could not be attributed to lack of knowledge of that particular structure.

To reduce testing time, the original 24 sentence types, each eight words long, used in pilot studies, were cut to twelve and twelve sets of 'eliciting' material prepared for the production tasks, in the third of Graham's studies.

The design of pictures used for each comprehension task was so controlled that the picking out by the child of one or two noticeable words would not do. The eliciting material was designed to allow guided conversation to steer the child towards his own production of that sentence type, as soon as he had divined the intentions of the tester. The vocabulary used and the pictured situation were kept within the knowledge of the child. Nursery school children, 'dull' primary school children, and children at ESN school participated.

The results showed that, although the ESN children's performance lagged badly for their age, they followed the normal pattern. Some showed they knew much more about the rules of language than would have been thought by hearing their everyday speech. There was a systematic relationship between their ability to perform and their span of immediate memory, showing that limits on the processing of sentences appear to be imposed by short-term memory. The observed deficit is therefore described as functional rather than structural in type. The short-term memory factor seems to be less important with 'dull' primary children.

An unexpected finding from Graham's investigation was the keen interest shown by the children in the experimental tasks, and the amount of learning which appeared to be taking place while the testing went on. Because of the speed with which children seemed to be able to produce sentences which they had not previously been able to say, this is probably an example of 'latent' learning, or the bringing out from the child's 'competence' into his 'performance' language structures which had been present in a previously unrealized form.

Using a similar method but original materials, Meers (1972) found that ESN(M) and ESN(S) children benefited from a large number of examples of twenty-four sentence types, when given daily practice. They became able to use sentence types which they had reduced to simpler forms when trying to repeat them in the earlier stages of the language practice. Children who had marked expressive language difficulty were able to indicate their level of understanding by a pointing response. While the materials used are not standardized against any other test, experience shows that the particular tasks are within the range of the normally developing five-year-old. So the repetition of sentences gives to the teacher a tool for a quick but reliable guide to what expressive language is available at that level. The speed and general style of tackling the three tasks helps in building up an all-round picture of the child's ability, and the types of errors which he makes can give valuable insights into his thinking processes. Errors tend either to change the meaning, or keep the meaning but simplify the structure, to reduce the meaning, or to mix together two sentence types. The important thing for the teacher is that the errors are not random, and are often overcome with surprising speed. This has its effect on the children's general level of confidence, resulting in increased spontaneity and a greater willingness to tackle new tasks, explore new areas of experience.

Through his investigations and the further work based on them, Graham has spotlighted the intertwined problems of the differing needs of groups of urban children, and of the different assessment by those engaged in compensatory programmes of what language remediation should consist of. Is it more and different vocabulary, or more practice with sentence structures which the children need? Is it the 'Handicapped' who need specific graded teaching? What is the language of the normal black child useful for, and in what areas does he need to have help in supplementing his family's styles of talk?

As we have seen, Labov bitterly opposes the notion of language deficit in the black child. He has an ally in Houston (1970), who regards language as a natural ability rather than a skill. She criticizes most investigations of language ability on the grounds that they only involve situations requiring the use of a 'school' register, which represents neither the whole of the child's performance nor his competence. Where a 'non-school' register can be elicited, and the child talks freely, 'natural linguistic creativity and frequent giftedness' are observed, resulting from the language games, verbal contests and narrative improvisations which are the forms of entertainment common to his social background.

Kochman (1964) analyzes this ability as it is used for social purposes. He describes it as highly oral-aural, it is the spoken skills which are highly prized. There are a number of terms — signifying, sounding, screaming, johning, ranking — for the game of verbal insults, generally known as 'playing the dozens'. Rapping, shucking, jiving, running it down, gripping, copping a plea (e.g. getting out of trouble) are other forms of verbal exhibitionism. Rapping may describe the art of story-telling in a fluent, highly personalized style, or it may be used as a name for a first approach to a young lady one wishes to know better; what we might term 'chatting up a bird'. 'Conning' means to manipulate people through the use of words; it is a means of controlling a hostile or threatening environment. 'Tomming' or 'Jeffing' is used to describe the role a negro may adopt before a white, to avert possible trouble; the deliberate adoption of a social stereotype of the 'Yass, sir, Mr Charlie, right away, Mr Charlie' type.

One can see how useful these types of language are in small-group behaviour. They can enforce group norms, decide status within the group, define inter-personal relationships, provide group-sanctioned modes of getting rid of hostility through teasing. They help to define and strengthen the group through the tongue-in-cheek fun that can be made of authority figures. They show striking similarities to social language used by working-class city white people. Compare 'conning' with our 'putting the poison down'; 'stirring it up' or 'making the bullets' (for other people to fire); 'rapping' as story telling with our 'canting', 'chewing the fat' (or rag); 'playing the dozens' with our 'slanging match', our 'codding' (a form of straight-faced humour of the leg-pulling kind) or 'Piliking' in Durham. I have already compared 'rapping' with 'chatting up a bird', and these cross-cultural similarities support the suggestion that these forms of verbal behaviour function to maintain group cohesion and resolve tensions in various urban societies.

Other forms of language play can be used to preserve the secrecy felt to be necessary for the in-group: back-slang, rhyming slang, riddles, certain types of regional jokes (e.g. the Black countryman poking straight faced fun at his own assumed 'thickness'). The use of proverbial sayings or interchanges ritualized by frequent use also defines attitudes. Children's jokes, riddles, singing games and skipping games are norms by which they assert their own culture and identity.

This richness and variety of socially useful styles of language illustrates the way that cultural groups express and elaborate concepts in ways which, though different, are equally valid.

For further evidence that language use in every type of community is fully developed to meet the needs of the people it serves; (a point of some importance when considering 'Black English', whether as it is used in the U.S.A. or the West Indies or in Britain) we can turn to Whorf's (1964) discussion of American, Indian and African language. He finds that:

. . . many American, Indian and African languages abound in finely wrought, beautifully logical discriminations about causation, action, result, dynamic or energic quality, directness of experience, etc., all matters of the function of thinking, indeed the quintessence of the rational. In this respect they far outdistance the European languages . . . (p 137)

Whorf was referring to such features as the availability of several past tenses, use of which not only depended on how long ago the past event took place, but also whether it continued to affect present events. But this does not deal with the criticism that such language uses particular rather than general terms. It is a point discussed by Boas (1964):

The fact that generalized forms of expression are not used does not prove inability to form them, but it merely proves that the mode of life of the people is such that they are not required; that they would however, develop just as soon as needed. (p 18)

Boas also applies this to the use of numerals for counting; e.g. the owner of a flock of sheep may know them individually by name and character, and does not necessarily want to count them. So lack of use of numerals beyond three does not mean inability to form the concepts of higher numbers. There are in the language of various tribes certain artificial, unidiomatic, abstract terms not used in ordinary speech, and these seem to correspond to terms such as 'essence' or 'existence', which we use in our language as devices for expressing the results of abstract thought, as in philosophy. Boas is claiming that language is moulded by cultural state, and changes as the cultural state changes. If he is right, then the effects of dialect, possible restricted language examples at home, or of a different language at home are not necessarily as bad as might be expected. In addition to the American material which is now plentiful, a study from New Zealand seems worth quoting (Clay, 1971). Four groups of children, from 'Professional' English background, 'Average' English background, those of Maori background who only spoke English, and those of Samoan background who were bi-lingual, were compared on tasks of sentence repetition, from age five to seven. Articulation, vocabulary, inflections, and sentence repetition abilities were all compared. Clay comments on the results:

When the New Zealand child enters school on his fifth birthday the child from a Professional home has a significant lead in sentence repetition skill over the Average English entrant. The latter gains in relative skill *over the first 18 months of schooling* so that the low but significant difference at five years was not found at later age. The improvement in the Average English group was more rapid in the first year of school than that of the Samoans so that a significant difference appears between these groups by six years. There were no statistically significant differences between Maori and Samoan groups, but there was a consistent tendency for differences to lessen with the monolingual Maori making rapid progress between five and a half and six years and bilingual Samoans improving at a faster rate than the Maori after six years. Overall, one is impressed with the steady, significant, and essentially parallel rate of increase in scores for every group over their level at school entry. (p 29–30)

And she adds:

Results . . . suggested that structural features of English sentences and interactions with behavioural strategies and mechanical limitations on processing information produce a sequence of difficulty at the ages studied which is only affected in minimal ways by experience with a different mother-tongue or dialect. (p 38)

Labov has said he does not regard the Bereiter and Engelmann programme itself as harmful but the consequences as dire; the teacher would hear what the child says, through the bias of 'deprivation' theory and his attitudes to the child become negative. Moreover, failure in this type of programme would be taken as indicative of something lacking in the children and their parents rather than in the theory and methods of the programme used.

As we have seen, much informed opinion is moving away from the 'verbal deprivation' concept, as it had been thought to affect whole ethnic or class groupings. While Bereiter and Engelmann aim to apply linguistic theory, they also confuse the issue through lack of clarity on theoretical and practical issues. Their emphasis on the language of instruction, while based on the positive idea that children can learn when they are provided with conceptual tools for doing so, is an oversimplification. The conceptual uses of language are treated as separate from and antecedent to social and imaginary uses.

Minuchin (1971) makes the point that young children are:

. . . not developmentally ready to learn to distinguish reality from fantasy, and they are not in the same kind of contact with reality as they will be as they grow older . . . we have regarded this shutting off of reality as an expression of creativeness. (p 81)

Chukovsky (1963) regards play with language as a delineation and confirmation of a concept through the notion of a joke; to appreciate the playful element in verbal comedy, one has to be aware of the correct relationship, and this verbal play is a way of objectifying the situation. Looked at in this way, using only instructional language, limits rather than develops conceptual and realistic thinking. It is not a question of one type or another type of language, for: 'With the help of fantasies, tall tales, fairy tales, and topsy-turvies of every type, children confirm their realistic orientation to reality' (p 113). Analysis of our familiar nursery rhymes confirm this. Consider just two examples. In *Boys and girls come out to play* compare the range and difficulty of the structures used, their subtlety and rhythm, with

Bereiter and Engelmann's 'this figure is triangular and big and green' and compare the reasoning and the sequential thinking involved in dealing with it; or in following Old Mother Hubbard through her adventures with her non-conformist dog. Or note the precise and exact imagery in children's playground chants:

Mrs White had a fright
In the middle of the night
She saw a ghost eating toast
Half-way up a lamppost.

The aim of the Bereiter and Engelmann programme of giving children the ability to process the concepts used in logical thinking can, in spite of Labov, be seen as good, in that they see the children are able and willing to learn. Gains in school success by the children confirm their point. Its weakness as a programme is that a limited number of structures are presented in a restricted way, and it appears to work with children who have already acquired language competence, and who have no deficit in such abilities as short term memory. The naive thinking behind the programme is shown in the belief that we can teach our slow learners prepositions by emphasizing them in the sentences we speak; normal intonational patterns are vital for carrying the feeling and a sense of meaning. The T.V. script-writer who gave staccato utterance to the Daleks knew what he was doing when he emphasized their non-humanity in this way. We need, with slow learners, to look deeper, take a less simplistic view of the nature of language and the roots of deficit. The formal neutrality of 'This figure is triangular and big and green' certainly has a place, later on, but to impose it at an early stage could lead to that rigidity we wish to avoid.

This is not what many teachers have been led to believe. It is not surprising that there is controversy over 'difference' or 'deficit', whether it is applied to black Americans or to black English children of West Indian origin; for language is bound up with our idea of ourselves. Critics of Creole languages seem unaware that these re-interpretations of a number of European languages beginning as 'Pidgin English', were developed by their users to provide the same linguistic resources as any other language. As Le Page (1966) points out, English has itself passed through a similar process in its time.

'Jargons' and 'Creole' need some explanation; they are terms which tend to be loosely used. Sometimes they are referred to as 'substitute' languages. Reinecke (1964) quotes Schultze's description: 'idioms which serve to bring about an incomplete understanding between men of different tongues'. (p 536) Reinecke distinguishes four classes:

1 Colonial Jargons.

2 Trade jargons.

3 Artificial auxiliaries – e.g. Esperanto.

4 Slaves and servants' languages.

Colonial jargon is used within an immigrant group; it is not used as a means of inter-group communication, and we are not concerned with it here.

Trade jargons are, and remain, supplementary languages. That is, both sets of people using them have a full language of their own; they tend to be short-lived expedients, often fluid and simple. They may have as few as 11,000 root words. They tend to disappear when trade relations are consolidated or changed into conquest relations.

Slave jargons, including Creoles, become primary languages. It is these with which we are concerned.

Where a small group of foreigners settle as colonists or traders in a much larger native population, they impose a simplified and corrupted form of their own language. But through intermarriage, domestic slavery, and religious conversion, the settlers acquire a part-native element. Idioms and words from the native language are thus introduced, leading to the formation of clearly defined local dialects. These remain in use with the mixed-blood groups, who mediate with the surrounding population in yet another trade-type jargon.

Plantation creole dialects resulted from the introduction of African slave labour to the tropics by Europeans. The dialects began as makeshift forms of communication between masters and their field hands, who in their turn taught the dialect to incoming slaves. The next stage was a levelling out and improving so that the slave dialect approached more nearly to their master's language. The white masters spoke Creole in domestic situations, that is in everyday intimate affairs where it became more expressive and graceful than, say, French. Though it was often regarded as a mark of social inferiority, it developed as language. As Reinecke says:

A new set of complexities was evolved; the Creole came to have its own 'inner essence' and to be applicable to social and religious concepts of considerable subtlety. (p 541)

And both white and coloured writers have produced Creole literature.

Sapir (1963) has, as we have seen, maintained that every known people 'speaks in the forms of a rich symbolic system' (p 42), going on to state:

The fundamental groundwork of language – the development of a clearcut phonetic system, the specific association of speech elements with concepts and the delicate provision for the formal expression of all manner of relations, all this meets us rigidly perfected and systematized in every language known to us.

Yet there is still a widespread belief that using slang terms, talking with a 'common' accent, or using grammatical forms considered to be deviant from those in fashionable use, are indicators of illiteracy, a low level of education, general ignorance, and a language system so cramped as not to allow for the development of abstract thinking. It is in this connection that the otherwise harmless word 'dialect', comes to mean not just 'difference' but 'inferiority'. It is not applied to the variety of language used by the high-status groups within a given society.

Children from the Indian sub-continent have a 'second' language learning problem, compounded when the mothers do not speak English, the fathers speak a heavily accented version, and habits of dress and diet which have become unsuitable in the new colder climate are retained. The younger the children are when they begin to learn their new language, the easier they find it; infants have little difficulty even without specific teaching. But the range they acquire in school may be restricted.

A growing number of Chinese children are now in schools, usually in small groupings in small towns. According to a pilot study (Jackson and Garvey 1974) the yearly intake is running at between 1,600 and 3,500. The needs of these children, their parents and teachers, seem to be just coming into our conscious awareness; the teaching method suggested, which includes finding out what the child knows, using leading questions, then taking it from there with an interchange of new information, seems a sensible approach to the practicalities of the situation.

Variations in dialect often are, though they need not be, associated with a sense of non-communication between the groups which make up the larger society. Whether they are or not depends not only on the amount of grammatical difference between them; it is the social ratings attached to the dialects, and the different purposes for which the dialect-using groups see language as being useful, that can lead to misunderstandings.

Menyuk (1971) lists the sociolinguistic factors involved, as:

1 The role and status of the speakers.

2 The environmental circumstances in which communication is taking place.

3 The purpose or function of the communication.

4 The topic and content of the communication.

Difficulties do arise when a wide range of grammatical and other rules are not the shared property of a language community. This suggests the need, in those communities where sub-groups live in near ghetto conditions, not only to create circumstances where experience of each other's styles of communication can be greatly increased, but also to level up standards of living for the deprived sub-group, so that opportunities can be better taken advantage of by the poor.

The terms 'high language' and 'low language' (in Dickie, 1968) which have been applied to disadvantaged children show that there is not one uniform group, with one basic language problem. And Gotkin (1968), writing of his own programmed instruction approach, says:

In reply to those who assert that ghetto children are not ready, the programme's orientation is sensible because it tests the dimensions of the 'lack of readiness'. What becomes obvious in challenging that assertion is that large proportions of ghetto children reveal themselves to be rapid learners and that the curriculum has failed to permit them to demonstrate how capable they are of learning. (p 34)

The preservation of a dialect use varying from that of the main community rests on social reasons rather than on lack of language ability. The social reasons include geographical distance, educational isolation from standard dialect speakers, social disapproval of friendships and marriages between members of different groups. The ways the non-standard speakers are spoken to when they use their dialects may also perpetuate differences since attitudes of contempt or punishment towards them may rouse their language loyalties. Dialect may be perceived as a means of maintaining the group's identity, together with its ethnic traditions, its religious and its cultural experiences.

The studies of sociolinguists, who have compared language use not only within communities, but across them, show how other people, and ourselves, use different aspects of language. I propose to look at some of the work in this field.

Fishman and Lueders-Salmon (1970) show that it is not necessarily a disadvantage to have a different type of verbal repertoire, if one lives in a stable community whose attitudes do not denigrate local dialect. In the district of Schwaben, where five or six varieties of Low German are used, there is not a conflict between this and the High German which children learn at school not as being more correct than their dialect, but as being more appropriate to certain contexts of use e.g., in singing, or in formal situations; so the contexts suitable for the use of their own variants are retained and added to. But within the community dialect users are not regarded as second class citizens.

The complexity of intertwined languages and their regional variations comes across in an example given by Fishman (1969) as he shows that people do not always use the same type of language to each other:

Government functionaries in Brussels who are of Flemish origin do not always speak Dutch *to each other* even when they all know Dutch *very* well and *equally* well. Not only are there occasions when they speak French to each other instead of Dutch, but there are some occasions when they speak standard Dutch and others when they use one or another regional variety of French with each other. Indeed, some of them also use different varieties of French with each other as well, one variety being particularly loaded with governmental officialese, another corresponding to the non-technical conversational French of highly educated and refined circles in Belgium, and still another being not only 'a more colloquial French' but the colloquial French of those who are Flemings. (p 47)

This question of when to say what to whom applies equally among people who are monolingual, and affects the way words are pronounced as well as the grammatical structure of what is said. Fishman's example of New Yorkers is that the same person who would sometimes say 'I sure hope yuz guys'll shut the lights before leavin', is also likely to say, or write, 'Kindly extinguish all illumination prior to vacating the premises.' One might add that in England, the Black countryman's 'Ow bin yer?' could at other times become 'How d'you do?'

Nor is this need to know what kind of things to say in what form, in what sort of situations to which people confined to complex urban societies. An account by Frake (1964) of the procedure to be followed when asking for a drink in Subanon (he describes the Subanon as 'pagan swidden agriculturalists') shows that social status is largely established through drinking encounters where skilled language use is a prized attribute. If the drinking continues long enough, says Frake, language play, with stylized song and verse competition, becomes a feature even of legal transactions:

Songs and verse are composed on the spot to carry on discussions in an operetta like setting . . . The most prestigious kinds of drinking songs require the mastery of an esoteric vocabulary by means of which each line is repeated with a semantically equivalent but formally different line . . . The Subanon drinking encounter thus provides a structured setting within which one's social relationships beyond one's everyday associates can be extended, defined, and manipulated through the use of terms of address, through discussion and argument and through display of verbal art. The most skilled . . . are the 'de facto' leaders of the society. (p 93)

The very frequent code-switching which takes place as people talk to each other also shows the exaggeration in the claim that the child of West Indian parentage is necessarily hampered in school because of differences between his grammar and vocabulary and that of the teachers.

Cross cultural experience is that the participants modify their language behaviour to understand and make themselves understood. Where child and teacher both do this, difficulties are likely to be partial and temporary rather than intractable. Gumperz (quoted by Pride 1970), in his study of the many village dialects in use in the Indian sub-continent, illustrates a similar process. The dialects form a continuous chain from Sind to Assam, so that adjacent areas understand each other, although widely separated areas do not. And switching between Hindi and Punjabi in Delhi, says Gumperz, gives rise to mixed styles of speech:

. . . which illustrate how language can seem to merge in 'stable bilingual communities' to the point at which it seems irrelevant to speak of 'interference' between distinct 'standard' forms of speech. (p 290)

Wight (1971) has described the effects of non-standard dialect, such as English-based Creole, on the child of West Indian parentage:

. . . in Britain the dialect speaking child is rarely restricted to a single dialect . . . Rather he starts at school to operate along a dialect continuum. (home, school, neighbourhood) . . . It is difficult otherwise to account for the speed and skill with which so many West Indian children acquire a more standard dialect for formal situations like school. (p 48)

This suggests that the teacher, while accepting the child's natural forms of speech, should make sure that his own instructions to the child are not so complex that the 'filter' of dialect difference prevents understanding; that the child should have plenty of opportunity to hear 'standard' English usage from other children as well as from the teacher.

The possibility of using both Patois and standard English in the school situation is discussed by Kirkaldy (1973). He gives an account of Patois in a Jamaican context which could be valuable to the teacher who wishes to try out language development ideas. Listening to stories is valuable, as standard English forms can be used by the child in writing without invidious comparisons. Written language is in any case different from spoken language. The confusion between written language and spoken language is linked in with the notion that there is one 'correct' form.

Bloomfield (1964) has examined this question and concludes:

There is no fixed standard of 'correct' English; one need only recall that no two persons speak alike, and that, taken as a whole, every language is constantly changing . . . All speaking, good or bad, is careless; only for a few moments at a time can one speak 'carefully' and when one does so, the result is by no means pleasing. (pp 391–2)

Bloomfield considers that we should describe only written forms as 'standard'. The spoken dialect forms which we bring to the written forms are socially characterized as 'bad', 'careless' etc.

The position is further complicated by the fact that what is 'standard' written English usage, becomes 'non-standard' as it is in time replaced by other 'standard' forms; and even punctuation use varies, with, for example, a more modern English style using fewer commas than in earlier prose. So criticisms of language forms in which superficial features are considered to be deviant may be quickly out-dated by the dynamics of the language process. The surface rules of a language are continuously restructured, as well as its sounds and its meanings. Different societies prize different aspects of language skill. Industrialized cultures place more relative emphasis on written language; much of the highly developed traditional English spoken skill was lost when cultural continuity was broken at the time of the Industrial Revolution. For example working conditions in factories often include a noise level and work discipline which precludes long conversations about unfamiliar subjects. This is only one of the reasons for the ritualization of social interchanges. A Monday morning conversation between a group of machine operators could run like this:

1st Operator 'Roll on half-past five'

2nd Operator 'Roll on Friday'

3rd Operator 'Roll on death'

4th Operator 'Oh, you're always wishing your lives away.'

To take this example as indicating the full range of language choices open to the individuals concerned, would be as serious a misrepresentation as is the myth of the poverty of expression of 'primitive' languages.

What it does indicate is that, as Labov (1969) points out, the study of language variation, as it occurs according to situation in all speech communities, is helpful to the understanding of language structure, the changes that take place within it, and the ways that 'significant choices within the set of possibilities open to the native speaker' (p 187) come to be made. This skill develops relatively late in the speaker's life. It is one expression of a system of underlying values. As such, it is a more widespread feature than we generally realize. Labov considers the four successive social groups which shape the individual's language, determine his competence in language use, and the complexity of his uses of speech. These are the family, the peer group, the school and the job.

While the family influences set the language process going, and as such are the primary source of language learning, a re-modelling to conform to pre-adolescent group types of speaking takes place. The skills which Labov describes as developing in American children; joke telling, rhymes, chants, songs, seem typical of the urban English child too, as the materials in the Opie's *Lore and Language of Schoolchildren* delightfully illustrate.

School styles emphasize care, formality in pronunciation, precise articulation. As the child learns to read, he may adjust his pronunciation to accommodate his new knowledge of how the word is spelled. His vocabulary embraces wider and differing uses. Although junior-age children make shifts in their style and usage according to context, it is not until their late teens that they usually become aware of the social stratification that is implied when someone says 'I ain't got no coat, I gorra gerit.'

The way that types of work affect language use is perhaps most clearly seen in the adoption of technical terms, and their use in a wider context. These may be vocabulary items only, or phrases and sayings which become proverbial e.g. 'I'm in my oil-tot'. Perhaps this is one reason for the rapid rate of linguistic evolution which takes place in cities. The group skills, or 'speech events' of the child's peer group, now reappear in adolescence and later life in a new guise. As before, skills are prized and evaluated. They provide means of placing the individual in his group, and of maintaining the cohesion of the group against whatever outside pressures may be operating.

The 'idiolect', or personal voice of any language user, his idiosyncratic use of it, must rest on the basis of the particular language variation or dialect he chooses. Differences between these variations have come about and are maintained in systematic ways; through geographical distance, ethnic barriers, the psychological distance between pre-adolescent and adolescent, the continuous language changes which run through whole regions, whole age levels. So pervasive are the effects of these unceasing changes within communities that it is unusual to find systematic language differences among speakers of the same age level in the same community who are in regular contact with one another. Therefore systematic differences can be taken to indicate a social discontinuity of some kind.

The difference between 'prestige' and 'non-prestige' forms, between 'standard' and 'non-standard' English is reinforced by an implied set of values associated with certain types of speech. When people still choose to use forms which they know carry a social stigma, it may be because first learned forms are by now so automatic as to be highly resistant to change; but it seems more likely that their deliberate use indicates a rejection of the values and rules of school or adult life. Other differences such as simplifying clusters of consonants occurring at the ends of words, the dropping of a final 'g' or 't', may not have any strong social value attached to them. They form part of a general tendency, that of making words easier to say.

This discussion of language use has touched upon some of the issues involved in the infinitely complex business of trying to make an assessment of language ability. It has necessitated discussion of the notion of deprivation, since the argument around what from the 'mainstream' standpoint is considered as 'deficit' and from the 'sub-culture' standpoint is considered as 'difference', has focused on language ability. The viewpoint adopted by Bereiter and Engelmann has determined the methods they have used in schools, and while such authors as Keddie (1973), Labov and Hymes (1972) consider the term deprivation to be more a device, a value judgement made from a middle-class standpoint, which is designed to hide the defects of schools.

Schools do have defects, but to regard the concept of deprivation as a myth is as misleading as considering all working class people as deprived. The denial of deprivation could be harmful if it were allowed to divert attention from the need to prevent the handicapping conditions which arise on the basis of deprivation and feed on poverty. There is a stratum where the cycle of poverty — lack of money, obsolete housing, poor clothing, inadequate food, insecurity, overcrowding, chronic illness, chemical pollutions, general lack of amenities at home, lack of knowledge about how to deal with the system, an overall feeling of hopelessness, lack of choices, powerlessness to alter any of this, add up to a considerable handicapping condition. Where a child from such a background has a weakness in any learning area — more likely with the premature, underweight babies that often result from the poor health of their overworked, overstressed mothers — his disability in that area of functioning will make it even harder for him to overcome the effects of the environment society has placed him in. This is a different case from the majority of urban dialect speaking children, though if the school regards his language, the language of his home, as something so crude that it must be eliminated, then 'difference' can be hardened into 'deficit' by this additional blow to his idea of himself.

We can apply this to our own expectations about the likely language abilities of children whose parents are immigrants, and I suggest we need to distinguish between the language performance of these children as it is heard in school and their concealed competence.

What we think of each other and of ourselves comes across in our language use, whether we will or no; even silence, the decision not to speak, can be highly revealing to the teacher. Because of language's unique ways of altering our ways of feeling and thinking, it may well be that giving many varieties and forms to the child and using many methods, 'structured' and 'unstructured', will be an effective means of ensuring that his idea of himself is positive; of helping the child to see himself as a rich source of ideas, as an inventive, resourceful, problem-solving person who can function successfully in personal relationships; at work; in his leisure; as a full member of his community.

7

Helping the hearing-impaired child in nursery or infant class

Now that more children with hearing impairment are diagnosed early, fitted with suitable hearing aids, and attend nursery schools or classes, there is an increasing number of children who, in spite of their hearing loss, can be educated in infant schools which do not have special facilities, other than an informed staff.

Having an informed staff, who understand that they can increase the amount and quality of the language information available to the child, may well be crucial for ensuring these children's educational progress. Their continued use of their hearing aids, their continuing efforts to make sense of language and to use it as a means of thinking, feeling, imagining and communicating, depend on the effectiveness of the measure we organise for them.

Sound is perceived as a result of the ear's response to the backward and forward vibrations of molecules in the air. The quicker or more frequent, these vibrations are, the higher the pitch of the sound produced. Pitch is measured in Hertz, and known as the frequency. So the greater the number of Hertz (Hz for short) the higher the sound or note. In speech sounds it is the vowels which fall into the higher frequency ranges.

The other important property of sound is its loudness, or intensity. In speech sounds, consonants usually have greater intensity than vowel sounds. Intensity is measured through a scale worked out in decibels (dbs for short). That point at which sound becomes detectable to a normally-hearing person is known as the threshold of sound. It is this threshold, not the absolute absence of sound, which gives the lowest reading, 0, on the decibel scale.

Hearing loss will affect the intensity of the sound as it is perceived, and the range of frequencies which are discernible. It will therefore affect such information-processing abilities as separating what is important, foreground voice-produced sound from unimportant background noise. This must be done before it is possible to organise speech sounds into meaningful sequences of words. In the classroom situation, even a small degree of hearing impairment may be transposed into a large degree of listening impairment. A twenty

140

decibel loss, for instance, is so mild that at home it is unlikely to interfere much with the reception and interpretation of speech. But in the usual conditions of a fair sized classroom it could lead to behaviour more consistent with a sixty decibel loss, which would cause severe interference with the acquisition of language skills. These problems of discriminating sounds would tend to reduce the child's attention. He would listen less. The teacher's task is to minimise such secondary effects arising on a primary disability.

Sight and hearing complement each other; they mediate between the inner needs of the self and those ideas of the world around us, which we build up through the information coming to us through our sense perceptions. So, as we listen to what others say, we watch for bodily position, facial expression, gestures, sound. The context in which the verbal message occurs gives considerable help in working out the meanings it conveys; it enables us to anticipate to know what subject matter to expect.

For the hearing impaired, visual clues take on even greater importance than for the normally-hearing. The talking adult's face should be turned towards the main light source in the room — perhaps a window — so that as much light as possible is falling on the speaker's face. Gesture or objects which are being used to help convey the meaning should be kept near the speaker's mouth, so that information from both gesture and lip-reading can be used at the same time, to supplement heard information. For instance, in speaking a message such as 'Give me the pen', in which the key word 'pen' cannot be lip-read because 'n' as a final consonant is not distinguishable, it would be useful to hold up a pen to show what is wanted; but if it is held at arm's length, the child has to choose between looking at the object and missing the instruction, or lip-reading the instruction and not knowing what he is to give. Clearly, the pen should be held close to the speaker's mouth, without obscuring the child's view of the lip movements.

Keeping the right distance when speaking to the child will help. If the child's loss is such that he is hearing sound more quietly than most, then either a somewhat louder voice, or coming a little closer, will bring an increased intensity of sound for the child. Speaking a little more slowly than usual, and as clearly as possible, will also be helpful provided that speech is not slowed down so much that the rhythmic flow, and the rise and fall of the voice, which carry so much language meaning, are lost. And as the aim is to enable children to understand language whoever uses it, they have to learn to adjust to a normal rate of speech delivery, if their lip-reading is to be functionally useful in everyday life.

Because of the importance of context clues, children should not be asked to discriminate single words. Nor should their own articulation be corrected before fluent speech is being used; oral failure may well result from this discouragement. Many opportunities for practice and repetition are needed, where the child can give language back in phrase or sentence form, using a conversational approach. Remember that in a situation where a group is talking together, the hearing-impaired child needs to be given clues to who is going to speak next, so that he does not lose lip-reading help through the time it takes to locate, and turn to see, the one who is the speaker.

The frustration arising from the misunderstandings of who is saying what about whom, may lead to outbursts of rage. These need to be met calmly by the teacher, whose reassuring attitude will be needed to reduce the child's feelings of anxiety or shame at his own behaviour. Encouragement to the child to take part in group activities, to develop imaginative play and the taking-on of the roles of significant others in play situations, will help to overcome some of the social immaturity shown by many hearing-impaired children. Some may have poor movement skills, if mechanisms controlling balance have been affected by damage to their ears. They may show the effects of a poor body-image in immature drawings of people; this should not be taken to indicate that such children necessarily have a low level of intelligence.

Where there is associated visual handicap, children should have glasses prescribed, be encouraged to wear these, and have them kept clean, well-fitting and in good repair. Frequent tests are advisable, since young children's eyesight may change rapidly.

The extra strain for the child, arising from his efforts of concentration on the clues needed for deciphering speech, will result in signs of fatigue, especially when a cold makes his hearing even worse, so allowances need to be made for this.

The child who is compensating for hearing loss by making extra use of vision for scanning the environment, will be more than usually sensitive to changes of level of light in the classroom. Similarly, he may be more sensitive to vibrations. These types of distraction can be avoided if we are aware of the problems they create. Again, because the hearing aid amplifies but cannot select significant from background sound, the child wearing a hearing aid is more vulnerable, more fatigued, in a noisy classroom. Noise can be reduced if one becomes aware of its sources. Tins or boxes which hold pencils, etc. can have their bases padded with a rim of foam plastic, so that there is no exaggerated bang when they are put down. Groups of children may learn to enjoy a game of picking up and putting down their chairs as quietly as possibly, rather than scraping their chairs along the floor in moving them from place to place. Where overalls are worn, cotton can be chosen in preference to rustling nylon ones. Curtains and carpeted areas can absorb echoes. Anticipating and avoiding sources of unpleasant noise may well prevent the situation where the child pulls off his hearing aid, and shows a marked reluctance to having it on again.

Skilled use of a hearing aid in varying conditions may take years to accomplish. We need to help the adaptation process by encouraging the child to wear the aid in as many circumstances as possible; this includes playtimes. Exceptions are very noisy situations such as echoing swimming baths, or times when immersion in water would ruin the aid. Spare parts for hearing aids should be available to schools through the peripatetic teachers who should be working with parents of very young children and bringing information and special teaching help into the schools where the children are placed.

All hearing aids are made up of a microphone, an amplifier, volume control and its switch; a lead to the receiver and ear mould; and batteries which supply the power. There are two main forms used by young children. The 'body aid', usually the Medresco OL 56, has microphone, amplifier and batteries within a plastic case, worn clipped to the child's jumper or outer clothing. The microphone grill must be unobstructed. A flexible lead connects this through thick and thin terminals fitted at each end, to the round plastic-backed receiver. This in turn clips on to the ear mould, an individually fitted and made plastic shape, with one small hole running through it, which is vital for transmitting sound into the affected ear (or to both ears if two aids are worn). The aid is switched on by the volume control. Many children with a mild or medium loss receive suitable help with the volume switch set at 3. If the aid should be accidentally switched off, and the correct setting is not known, this is a 'safe' setting to use as a temporary measure.

The Medresco OL67 is a smaller aid worn behind the ear. Again, the plastic case houses microphone, amplifier and a small circular battery. A short stiff lead links the aid to the receiver, with thick and thin pins so that it can only be put in correctly. This aid has a three-position switch. '0' indicates the off position, 'M' amplified sound, and 'T' is provision for when a special listening coil is switched on, cutting out the microphone. This aid will normally be set at 'M' for daily use. The volume can be adjusted by turning a wheel near the top of the aid; pushing this downwards increases the volume.

It is advisable to make a daily check on the working of the aid. When it is off the child, but switched on, with the volume control near maximum, a whistling noise should be heard when the receiver is moved to and fro about twelve inches from the rest of the aid. If no sound can be heard, a new battery may be needed, or it may need to be re-located. If the sound heard is intermittent, the fault may be in the lead. A child's playground fall often results in a cracked receiver, and this, like the lead, is easily replaced. The code number on the replacement should be the same as that on the old receiver.

The ear mould is vital, and should be gently cleaned with warm soapy water to clear any wax from the hole. When putting the mould back in the child's ear, pull the lobe of the ear down, and make sure that the mould fits firmly into the ear. If there is any gap between ear and mould, the child will suffer from the feedback whistle we hear when the aid is being tested.

Any sounds which we want the child to hear well should be made near the microphone. It is the near sounds which will be the most amplified. So we need to re-train our own habits, adapt to make the best use of the child's aids to hearing. Imagination is our aid here. Anyone concerned with the child's education must consider how things seem to the child, how he is interpreting situations and events in the light of his previous experiences. Even the best of well-maintained aids will not replace the understanding and the encouragement we give to efforts made by the child to develop the language ability we can so easily take for granted.

8
Afterword

I have tried to give a broad picture of language learning, as it arises on the basis of the child's pre-language constructs. I have presented a view of the child as an active information-processor, model builder, and problem solver. I have taken the view that language acquisition is based on species-specific abilities which are realized through appropriate stimulation.

In discussing the different ways that language is used, I have wanted to show these things:

1 Language is needed to develop and refine modes of feeling, thinking, imagining, and experiencing, which start to establish themselves at the pre-language baby stage.

2 Language is a means of discovering who one is, and where one fits into the family and into society.

3 That all known languages are fully developed systems, responsive to the needs of the communities using them, and helping to shape the particular forms of consciousness of their users.

4 That the social contexts of language use indicate that variants are a common feature. That these variants are selected according to the situations and the persons involved.

5 That sub-cultural dialect use need not be seen as a sign of social disadvantage. That it is the type of community in which its use occurs that determines whether dialects are regarded as something to be eradicated, or as acceptable in certain contexts, provided they are supplemented by the dialect of the main culture.

6 That language change is continually proceeding in a regular fashion. There is not a fixed unchanging 'standard' form of any language.

7 That it is both possible and desirable to give children a range of all forms, dialects, vocabularies, styles, tones.

8 That the fuller the range of language uses and styles available to

the speaker, the greater the number of informed choices that are open to him; thus he is able to influence his environment as well as knowing himself to be subject to its laws.

In showing how the language handicapped child can and should be helped towards realizing these aims within the educational system, my aim has been not so much to lay down rules or set procedures as to encourage the teacher to look at the problems in a number of alternative ways. New insights into old problems can come from an extension of our knowledge, when this is coupled with the flexibility of attitude that makes for willingness to reconsider. Recombining and reconsidering are themselves greatly helped by the formulating power of language; as Hotopf (1965) puts it, 'one may be surprised and interested by the things one finds oneself saying' (p 275), and I have found this to be equally true of what one writes.

I have referred to, quoted, and drawn on ideas from a wide field. My last quotation, illustrating among other things the effective use of the double negative, comes from the closing words of *The Adventures of Huckleberry Finn*. I use it for the devastating accuracy with which it states my present feelings:

. . . there ain't nothing more to write about, and I am rotten glad of it, because if I'd a knowed what a trouble it was to make a book I wouldn't a tackled it and ain't a-going to no more.

I hope that what I have written will be of some practical use to teachers.

Appendix

This is intended to suggest a method of considering the general aims of the broad language programme taking place within the classroom, and how these aims might be made more specific by a statement of the desired objectives at given stages, together with the material provision thought to be needed for the realization of the specific objectives.

It will be seen that the left hand column which deals with the desired behaviour, begins at an early level of functioning which includes motor skills, and works through to a stage where the child can function at quite a high level and possesses a variety of concepts based on many different kinds of experience. The abilities named do not necessarily always appear in the order listed, and where there is physical handicap may not be acquired at all. But it is useful to have some statement of abilities involved in, or helpful to, the language process. By using it as a checklist, it can spotlight areas of strength or weakness, so indicating to the teacher what to do and what to aim at next.

The right hand column consists of the substance of the provision through which it is hoped to reach forward to what is new and desirable in the child's development. Much of the equipment listed is common currency of nursery and infant school; but it is not a bad exercise for a teacher to consider what is wanted in the classroom and why it is wanted. In this connection one might paraphrase an axiom of William Morris, and have nothing in the classroom which one does not know to be useful or believe to be beautiful.

My suggestions for curriculum planning are meant as a springboard, a starting point only, and should be added to and altered as teaching experience exposes gaps or errors in the thinking that has gone into them.

CURRICULUM PLANNING AS APPLIED TO LANGUAGE ACQUISITION

Aim: to develop fluent and appropriate language skills

General objectives

Behavioural components

Competence in the following areas:
Motor skills
Selective attention
Perceptions
Integration of perceptions
Imagery
Symbolic play
Simple concept formation
Memory skills
Listening skills
Social interaction skills
Ability to use gesture
Understanding spoken language
Producing sentences, simple to complex
Adequate vocabulary
Clear articulation
Thinking skills
Range of language styles

Substantive components

Nursery/infant provision
and experiences to cover
as wide a range as
possible, plus informed
individualized teaching of
skills, using the
additional help of
specific schemes

Specific objectives

Behavioural

Directing attention to the following areas:
Ability to suck, blow, chew, lick
Ability to make comfort and discomfort sounds,
  calls, crying, shrieking
Following an object by eye, reaching for and
  grasping it
Smiling, laughing. Sitting up unaided
Turning head in direction of heard sound
Anticipating consequences of heard sound
Knowing familiar from unfamiliar people
Response to facial expressions, gestures
Picking up small object with thumb-finger
  opposition
Concept of permanence of object
Ability to crawl, stand up, walk
Symbolic play with toys – pretending
Expressive sounds, vowels, consonants, phonetic
  contrasts, babbling
Physical response to words in context
Response to simple comments, mainly through
  gesture, e.g. 'Wave by-by'
Vocal play. Self-listening
Listening to environmental sounds, sounds made
  by other people
Imitation of sounds made by others

Substantive

Large and small play
  material: bikes, trolleys,
  climbing frames, large
  and small balls, skipping
  ropes, hoops, etc. (to
  promote gross and fine
  motor development)
Dressing up materials,
  sand, water, shop,
  Wendy house, domestic
  play materials, table
  games, construction kits,
  jigsaw puzzles, puppets,
  telephone
Books: nursery rhymes,
  poetry, information,
  simple dictionaries,
  picture and story books
  within child's experience,
  expanding child's
  experience and outside
  his experience in fantasy
  and 'fairy' tales, giants,
  witches, trolls, animals

Behavioural	Substantive
Use of calls and sounds to modify environment, bringing and getting people to know what he wants and to do it for him	Crayons, pencils, paints, paper of various types, colour, size and shape
Use of gesture for these purposes	Tracing paper
Use of gesture and sounds together for these purposes	'Odds and ends' for
Increased understanding of verbal utterances, becoming less dependent on context	classifying, making models etc.
Use of combined sounds, and words	Musical instruments
Running, jumping, kicking of ball	Outings, trips, expeditions
'Jargon' sounds strung together in intonational patterns suggestive of meaning	Adults, (including men) Children – same age and
Can point to own features on request	older
One word used as if it is a sentence – sentence used as if giant word	Development schemes Assessment materials
Points to object to learn its name	Teaching programmes
Two word sentences, primitive grammar	Reading schemes
Three word sentences, primitive grammar	Infant method

Use of 'No' added to simple sentence
'What' questions to get confirmation
Sentences with 'telegraphese'; function words omitted
'Wh' questions as enquiries
Larger sentences. Inflected endings
Use of overgeneralized rules
'What', 'Who' and 'Where' questions extending to 'Why'
'Tag' questions, e.g. 'isn't it'
'No' used in 'correct' place in sentence and concept of 'No'
Approximation to adult grammar
Increase in complexity of structures, length of sentences
Some embedded bases
Selective attention in response to verbal instructions
Understanding without benefit of context clues or gesture
Response to implication of a direction, e.g. 'It's dinner-time' – child goes to wash hands
Response when instruction is opposed to situation
Enjoyment of nonsense, makes up songs and rhymes
Jumping, climbing, balancing, hopping, skipping (without rope)
Throwing and catching large balls
Cutting out
Begins to separate word from its referent
Interprets pictures
Draws pictures – scribble, simple stereotypes, objects disposed on paper in random arrangement, copies shapes. Does simple jig-saw puzzles, constructs play objects, builds complex structures with bricks etc.
Draws and paints organized pictures, provides language commentaries on them
Ability to trace

Behavioural

Figure-ground differentiation. Can find 'hidden' objects in pictures

Able to arrange pictures in sequence that tells story

Plays alongside and sometimes with others

Mimes common actions. Dramatic play, fantasy play

Carries out verbal instructions of increasing complexity

Listens to a told story or rhyme

Answers questions on a told story

Tells a known story, with picture cues

Chats with others. Replies relevantly to their remarks and questions

Use of 'and' extends its meaning to 'and subsequently' and 'and previously'

Concept of time expressed with words implying time relationships, before/after while, when

Asks all questions. Finds out about things

Can tell people things, tell them what to do

Can use language to mediate a task, i.e. by repeating instructions to himself as he performs it, and as an aid to memory

Can describe a past experience, describe objects in their absence

Concepts involving relative ideas – think, might, ought, should, some, bigger than, smaller than, more than, less than

Can forecast a future event 'I think it's going to rain'

Articulates clearly enough to be readily understood

Begins to manage consonant strings: 'school', 'drinks', 'crisps'

Understands language concepts needed for reading, e.g. word, letter, sentence, space

Word recognition. Play with letter shapes

Letter-sound correspondence

Identifies objects which go together, e.g. cup and saucer

Has a knowledge of constraints in language use, i.e. knows which words are likely to follow what

Can speak suitably to different people in a variety of circumstances

Can discriminate sounds, e.g. final and initial consonants, middle sounds

Can discriminate musical tone, pitch, volume

Has sense of rhythm, sequencing, pattern, in listening to and making music, singing

Eye-hand co-ordination, sense of direction, left to right eye movements

Classification skills – groups by colour, shape, size, thickness, texture

Able to perform multiple classification tasks

Knows some superordinate categories, e.g. food, toys

Understands and accepts simple rules of games. Skips or tries to with rope

Behavioural

Has functionally useful concepts of up/down,
 top/bottom, same/different, big-bigger-biggest,
 small-smaller-smallest, more/less, rough/smooth,
 lighter/heavier, straight/curved, before/after. Can use
 these in simple cause and effect reasoning
Ability in cross-modal coding — can recognize
 material presented through one sensory channel,
 and interpret it through a different sensory mode
Ability to read simple material with understanding
Uses 'because' in what he says. Can complete a
 sentence, e.g. 'He did it because'
Uses 'while' in what he says
Can complete a sentence with 'while'. 'He played
 while . . .'
Can define 'because', in his own terms
Uses 'although'. Can complete a sentence using
 'although . . .'
Can define 'although', in his own terms
Uses concept of future to be able to wait for a
 reward, a turn, or a desired event
Can find his way about neighbourhood, can be
 trusted to do so, for shopping, play, etc.

Bibliography

Barnes, K.H.J. (1970) *Language and the Mentally Handicapped.* North Berks Society for Mentally Handicapped.

Barnes, K.H.J. (1970) 'A Foundation of Language', in *Special Education* 59–60 June 1970.

Bereiter, C. and S. Engelmann (1966) *Teaching Disadvantaged Children in the Pre-School.* Prentice-Hall, Englewood Cliffs.

Bernstein, B. and D. Henderson (1969) 'An Approach to the Study of Language and Socialization', in *The Ecology of Human Intelligence* ed. L. Hudson. Penguin Books (1970).

Bernstein, B. (1970) 'Social Class, Language and Socialization', in *Language and Social Context* ed. P.P. Giglioli. Penguin Books (1972).

Bernstein, B. (1972) 'A Critique of the Concept of Compensatory Education', in *Functions of Language in the Classroom* ed. C.B. Cazden, V.P. John, D. Hymes. Teachers College Press, Columbia University, New York.

Bizzi, E. (1974) 'The Co-ordination of Eye-Head Movements', in *Scientific American* vol 231, 4 pp 100–110.

Blakemore, C. (1974) *Modern Problems in Paediatrics* vol 13 p 229, quoted in 'Monitor', *New Scientist* vol 64 no 918.

Blank, M. and F. Solomon (1968) 'A Tutorial Programme to develop Abstract Thinking in Socially Disadvantaged Children', in *Child Development* 39 pp 37–9.

Bloom, L. Hood, L. and P. Lightbown (1974) 'Imitation in Language Development: If, When and Why', in *Cognitive Psychology* vol 6 no 3 pp 380–421.

Bloomfield, L. (1964) 'Literate and Illiterate Speech', in *Language in Culture and Society* ed. D. Hymes. Teachers College Press, Columbia University, New York.

Boas, F. (1964) 'Linguistics and Ethnology', in *Language in Culture and Society* ed. D. Hymes. Teachers College Press, Columbia University, New York.

Braine, M.D.S. (1971) 'The Acquisition of Language in Infant and Child', in *The Learning of Language* ed. C.E. Reed. Appleton-Century-Crofts, New York.

Brannon, B.J. Jnr. (1968) 'A Comparison of Syntactic Structures in the Speech of three and four-year-old Children', in *Language and Speech* vol 11 p 171.

Brottman, M.A. ed. (1968) *Language Remediation for the Disadvantaged Pre-School Child.* Monograph of Society for Research in Child Development vol 33, 8. University of Chicago Press, Chicago.

Brown, R. (1958) *Words and Things.* The Free Press, Glencoe.

Brown, R. (1968) 'The Development of Wh. Questions in Child Speech', in *Journal of Verbal Learning and Verbal Behaviour* vol 7 pp 279–90.

Bruner, J. (1966) *Towards a Theory of Instruction*. Harvard University Press, Cambridge, Mass.

Byers, P. and H. Byers (1972) 'Non-verbal Communication and the Education of Children', in *Functions of Language in the Classroom* ed. C.B. Cazden, V.P. John, D. Hymes. Teachers College Press, Columbia University, New York.

Campbell, R. and R. Wales (1970) 'The Study of Language Acquisition', in *New Horizons in Linguistics* ed. J. Lyons. Penguin Books.

Carter, D.B. (1970) 'Vision and Learning Disorders', in *Interdisciplinary Approaches to Learning Disorders* ed. D.B. Carter. Chilton Book Company, Philadelphia.

Cass, J. (1971) *The Significance of Children's Play*. Batsford, London.

Cazden, C.B. (1972) *Child Language and Education*. Holt, Rinehart and Winston Inc., New York.

Chaloner, L. (1963) *Feeling and Perception in Young Children*. Tavistock Press. London.

Chomsky, N. (1967) 'Recent Contributions to the Theory of Innate Ideas', in *The Ecology of Human Intelligence* ed. L. Hudson. Penguin Books (1970).

Chomsky, N. (1968) 'Linguistic Contributions to the Study of Mind: Future', in *Language in Thinking* ed. P. Adams. Penguin Books (1972).

Chukovsky, K. (1963) *2–5*. University of California Press, Berkeley.

Cicourel, A.V. (1973) *Cognitive Sociology*. Penguin Education.

Clarke, E.V. (1973) 'How Children Describe Time and Order', in *Studies of Child Language and Development* ed. C.A. Ferguson and D.I. Slobin. Holt, Rinehart and Winston Inc., New York.

Clausen, J.A. (1966) 'Family Structure, Socialization and Personality', in *Review of Child Development Research* vol 2. ed. M.L. Hoffman and L.W. Hoffman. Russell Sage Foundation, New York.

Clay, M.M. (1971) 'Sentence Repetition. Elicited Repetition of a Controlled Set of Syntactic Structures by Four Language Groups', in *Society for Research in Child Development* vol 43 no 136 p 3. University of Chicago Press, Chicago.

Collard, R.R. (1971) 'Social and Play Behaviours of Infants reared in an Institution and in Lower- and Middle-Class Homes', in *Child Development* vol 42 pp 1003–15.

Cowan, P.A. (1970) 'The Nature of Psychological-Educational Diagnosis', in *Interdisciplinary Approaches to Learning Disorders* ed. D.B. Carter. Chilton Book Company, Philadelphia.

Cratty, B.J. and M.M. Martin (1969) *Perceptual-Motor Efficiency in Children*. Lea and Febiger, Philadelphia.

Davie, R. Butler, N. and H. Goldstein (1972) *From Birth to Seven*. National Children's Bureau, Longman.

Davis, K. (1967) *Human Society*. Collier Macmillan, London.

Danziger, K. (1971) *Socialization*. Penguin Education.

Dickie, J.P. (1968) 'Effectiveness of Structured and Unstructured (Traditional) Methods of Language Training', in Brottman (1968).

Douglas, J.W.B. (1964) *The Home and the School.* McGibbon and Kee, London.

Engel, R.C. (1968) *Language Motivating Experiences for Young Chlidren.* D.F.A. Publishers, Los Angeles.

Erikson, E.H. (1965) *Childhood and Society.* Penguin Books.

Ervin-Tripp, S. (1971) 'Social Background and Verbal Skills', in *Language Acquisition: Models and Methods* ed. R. Huxley and E. Ingram. Academic Press, London.

Evans, D. (1974) 'Language Development in Mongols', in *Special Education: Forward Trends* vol 1, 4.

Fishman, J.A. (1969) 'The Sociology of Language', in *Language and Social Context* ed. P.P. Giglioli. Penguin Books (1972).

Fishman, J.A. and E. Lueders-Salmon (1970) 'What has the Sociology of Everyday Life to say to the Teacher?', in *Understanding Everyday Life* ed. J.D. Douglas. Aldine Publishing Co.

Frake, C.O. (1964) 'How to Ask for a Drink in Subanon', in *Language and Social Context* ed. P.P Gigioli. Penguin Books (1972).

Gaines, R. (1970) 'A New Look at Perceptual Development', in *Interdisciplinary Approaches to Learning Disorders* ed. D.B. Carter. Chilton Book Co., Philadelphia.

Garn, S.M. (1966) 'Body Size and its Implications', in *Review of Child Development Research* vol 2 ed. M.L. Hoffman and L.W. Hoffman. Russell Sage Foundation, New York.

Gotkin, L.G. (1968) 'Programmed Instruction as a Strategy for Developing Curricula for Disadvantaged Children', in Brottman (1968).

Graham, N.C. (1968) 'Short Term Memory and Syntactic Structure in E.S.N. Children', in *Language and Speech* p 209.

Graham, N.C. (1970) *Some Aspects of the Language Disabilities of E.S.N. Children. A Psycholinguistic Approach,* unpublished Ph.D. Thesis, University of Birmingham.

Gray, S. et al (1966) *Before First Grade.* Teachers College Press, New York.

Greene, J. (1972) *Psycholinguistics, Chomsky and Psychology.* Penguin Education·

Greenfield, P. Reich, L. and R. Olver (1966) 'On Culture and Equivalence', in *Language in Thinking* ed. P. Adams. Penguin Books (1972).

Griffiths, R. (1935) *Imagination in Early Childhood.* Routledge and Kegan Paul, London.

Gulliford, R. (1960) 'Teaching the Mother Tongue to Backward and Subnormal Pupils', in *Educational Research* 11, 2 pp 82–100.

Gulliford, R. (1971) *Special Educational Needs.* Routledge and Kegan Paul, London.

Haber, R.M. and M. Hershenson (1973) *The Psychology of Visual Perception.* Holt, Rinehart and Winston Inc., New York.

Halliday, M.A.K. (1969) 'Relevant Moαels of Languages', in *Educational Review* 22, 1 pp 26–38.

Halliday, M.A.K. (1970) 'Language Structure and Language Function', in *New Horizons in Linguistics* ed. J. Lyons. Penguin Books.

154

Halsey, A.H. ed. (1972) *Educational Priority vol 1. E.P.A. Problems and Policies.* HMSO, London.

Hart, N.W.M. (1968) *Psycholinguistic Research in Queensland Schools.* Department of Education, Queensland Bulletin no 34, 1961–66.

Hewett, F. (1964) 'A Hierarchy of Educational Tasks for Children with Learning Disorders', in *Exceptional Children* 34, 4 pp 207–14.

Hockett, C.F. (1960) 'The Origin of Speech', in *Scientific American* vol 203 pp 89–96.

Hopper, R. and R.C. Naremore (1973) *Children's Speech.* Harper and Row, New York.

Hotopf, W.H.H. (1965) *Language, Thought and Comprehension.* Routledge and Kegan Paul, London.

Houston, S.H. (1970) 'A Re-examination of some Assumptions about the Language of the Disadvantaged Child', in *Child Development* vol 41 pp 947–61.

Hunt, J.McV. (1961) *Education and Experience.* Ronald Press, New York.

Hunt, J.McV. (1968) 'Environment, Development and Scholastic Attainment', in *Social Class, Race and Psychological Development.* Holt, Rinehart and Winston Inc., New York.

Hymes, D. (1972) 'Introduction', in *Functions of Language in the Classroom* ed. C.B. Cazden, V.P. John, D. Hymes. Teachers College Press, Columbia University, New York.

Ingram, T.T.S. (1972) 'The Classification of Speech and Language Disorders in Young Children', in *The Child with Delayed Speech* ed. M. Rutter and J.A.M. Martin. Heinemann, London.

Jackson, B. and A. Garvey (1974) *Chinese Children.* National Education Development Trust, Cambridge.

John, V.P. and S. Moskovitch (1970) 'Language Acquisition and Development in Early Childhood', in *Linguistics in School Programs Part II* ed. A.H. Marckwardt. University of Chicago Press, Chicago.

Jones, M.V. ed. (1972) *Language Development.* Charles C. Thomas, Springfield.

Kagan, J. (1967) 'On the Need for Relativism', in *The Ecology of Human Intelligence* ed. L. Hudson. Penguin Books (1970).

Kagan, J. (1971) *Understanding Children: Behaviour, Motives and Thought.* Harcourt Bruce, Jovanovitch, New York.

Karnes, M.B. (1968) *Helping Young Children Develop Language Skills.* Council for Exceptional Children, Arlington.

Keddie, N. (1973) *Tinker-Tailor . . . The Myth of Cultural Deprivation.* Penguin Books.

Kessel, F.S. (1970) *The Role of Syntax in Children's Comprehension from ages 6 to 12.* Monograph of the Society for Research in Child Development no 139 vol 135 no 6. University of Chicago Press, Chicago.

Kircaldy, J. (1973) 'Patois, Education and Jamaica', in *New Society* 4 October 1973.

Kirk, S.A. (1968) 'Illinois Test of Psycholinguistic Abilities: its Origins and Implications for Learning Disorders', in *Special Child Publications* vol 3 ed. J. Hellmuth.

Kochman, T. (1964) 'Black American Speech Events and a Language Program for the Classroom', in *Functions of Language in the Classroom* ed. C.B. Cazden, V.P. John, D. Hymes. Teachers College Press, Columbia University, New York.

Krekling, S. and P. Anderson (1974) 'Visual Performance of Children in Norwegian Special Schools', in *British Journal of Physiological Optics* vol 28 no 3 (1973) pp 49–160.

Labov, W. (1969) 'The Logic of Non-standard English', in *Language and Social Context* ed. P.P. Giglioli. Penguin Books (1972).

Labov, W. (1972) 'The Study of Language in its Social Context', in *Language and Social Context* ed. P.P. Giglioli. Penguin Books (1972).

Lenneberg, E.H. (1967) *Biological Functions of Language.* J. Wiley and Sons, New York.

Le Page, R.B. (1966) *Linguistic Problems of West Indian Children in English Schools.* Report by the Community Relations Commission 1970 of speech made to the Educational Panel of Commonwealth Immigrants.

Lewin, R. (1974) 'The Poverty of Undernourished Brains', in *New Scientist* vol 64 pp 268–74.

Lewis, M.M. (1963) *Language, Thought and Personality.* George Harrap and Co., London.

Luria, A.R. (1960) 'The Role of Speech in the Formation of Temporary Connections and the Regulation of Behaviour', in *Educational Psychology in the USSR.* ed. B. Simon. Routledge and Kegan Paul, London (1963).

McNeill, D. and M.B. McNeill (1973) 'What does a Child Mean When He Says No?', in *Studies of Child Language Development* ed. C.A. Ferguson and D.I. Slobin. Holt, Rinehart and Winston Inc., New York.

Mead, G.H. (1934) *Mind, Self and Society.* University of Chicago Press, Chicago.

Meers, H.J.A. (1972) *A Teaching Programme for Improving the Language Performance of Slow-learning Children.* Dissertation University of Birmingham School of Education.

Menyuk, P. (1971) *The Acquisition and Development of Language.* Prentice-Hall, Engelwood Cliffs.

Miller, G.W. (1971) *Educational Opportunity and the Home.* Longman, London.

Mills, M. and E. Melhuish (1974) 'Recognition of Mother's Voice in Early Infancy', in *Nature* vol 252 p 123.

Minuchin, P. and B. Biber (1968) 'A Child Development Approach to Language in the Pre-School Disadvantaged Child', in Brottman (1968).

Minuchin, P. (1971) 'Correlates of Curiosity and Exploratory Behaviour in Pre-School Disadvantaged Children', *Child Development* vol 42 no 3 pp 939–49.

Mittler, P. (1972) 'Psychological Assessment of Language Abilities' and 'Language Development and Mental Handicaps', in *The Child with Delayed Speech* ed. M. Rutter and J.A.M. Martin. Heinemann Medical, London.

Molloy, J.S. (1965) *Teaching the Retarded Child to Talk.* U.L.P., London.

Murphy, K. (1972) 'Attention and Feedback', in *The Child with Delayed Speech* ed. M. Rutter and J.A.M. Martin. Heinemann Medical, London.

Nelson, K. (1973) *Structure and Strategy in Learning to Talk*. Monograph of Society for Research in Child Development no 149. University of Chicago Press, Chicago.

Opie, I. and P. Opie (1960) *The Lore and Language of Schoolchildren*. Clarendon Press, Oxford.

Osborn, J. (1968) 'Teaching a Language to Disadvantaged Children', in Brottman (1968).

Piaget, J. (1971) *Mental Imagery and the Child*. Routledge and Kegan Paul, London.

Pride, J.B. (1970) 'Sociolinguistics', in *New Horzions in Linguistics* ed. J. Lyons. Penguin Books.

Reinecke, J.E. (1964) 'Trade Jargons and Creole Dialects as Marginal Languages', in *Language in Culture and Society* ed. D. Hymes. Teachers College Press, Columbia University, New York.

Renfrew, C.E. (1972) *Speech Disorders in Children*. Pergamon Press, Oxford.

Sapir, E.C. (1963) *Language*. Hart-Davis, London.

Sampson, O.C. (1958) 'A Study of Speech Development in Children 18–30 Months', in *British Journal of Educational Psychology* vol 26 no 3 p 194.

Schliefelbusch, R.L. Copeland, R.H. and J.O. Smith eds. (1967) *Language and Mental Retardation*. Holt, Rinehart and Winston Inc., New York.

Skinner, B.F. (1957) *Verbal Behaviour*. Appleton-Century-Crofts, New York.

Smith, H.P. and L.E.V. Dechant (1961) *Psychology in Teaching Reading*. Prentice-Hall, Englewood Cliffs.

Speier, M. (1970) 'The Everyday World of the Child', in *Understanding Everyday Life* ed. J.D. Douglas. Aldine Publishing Co.

Watson, P. (1972) 'Can Racial Discrimination Affect I.Q.?', in *Race, Culture and Intelligence* ed. K. Richardson and D. Spears. Penguin Books.

Whorf, B.L. (1964) 'A Linguistic Consideration of Thinking in Primitive Communities', in *Language in Culture and Society* ed. D. Hymes. Teachers College Press, Columbia University, New York.

White, B.L. (1971) *Human Infants' Experience and Psychological Development*. Prentice-Hall, Englewood Cliffs.

Wight, J. (1971) 'Dialect in School', in *Educational Review* vol 24 no 1 pp 47–59.

Woodward, M.W. (1971) *The Development of Behaviour*. Penguin Books.

Vygotsky, L.S. (1962) *Thought and Language*. M.I.T. Press.

Yule, W. and M. Berger (1972) 'Behaviour Modification Principles and Speech Delay', in *The Child with Delayed Speech* ed. M. Rutter and J.A.M. Martin. Heinemann Medical, London.

Index

Jones, M.V., 38, 109
Kagan, J., 12, 59, 64
Karnes, M.B., 122
Keddie, N., 138
Kessel, F.S., 56–7
Kircaldy, J., 135
Kirk, S.A., 120
Knoblock, 117
Kochman, T., 107, 126
Krekling, S., 42

Labov, W., 88, 109, 110–12, 126, 129, 130, 136–7, 138
Lenneberg, E.H., 24, 26, 37, 43
Le Page, R.B., 130
Lewin, R., 117
Lewis, M.M., 35
Lilienfeld, 117
Lovaas, 124
Lovitt, 124
Lueders-Salmon, E, 133
Luria, A.R., 59

McNeill, D., 46, 56
Martin, M.M., 8, 11
Maed, G.H., 76, 91–3
Meers, H.J.A., 125
Melhuish, E., 35, 63
Menyuk, P., 22, 113, 124, 132
Miller, G.W., 2, 61, 91
Mills, M., 35, 63
Minuchin, P., 15, 109, 114, 129
Mittler, P., 43, 120–1, 123
Molloy, J.S., 10, 119
Moskovitch, S., 107
Murphy, K., 39, 52

Naremore, R.C., 113
Nelson, K., 31–3, 44, 46, 61, 75

Opie, I. and P., 137
Osborn, J., 107–9
Osgood, 24, 120

Pasamanick, 117
Piaget, J. 15, 28–9, 30, 34, 53, 55, 58
Pride, J.B., 135

Reinecke, J.E., 130–1
Renfrew, C.E., 10, 122

Sampson, O.C., 3
Sapir, E.C., 30, 107, 131
Schliefelbusch, R.L., 44
Skinner, B.F., 24
Smale, J., 108
Smith, H.P., 117

Solomon F., 118
Speier. M., 62–3, 91
Spradlin, 123
Swift, Jonathan, 22, 23

Turner, 78

Vygotsky, L.S., 51, 55–6, 58, 59, 92

Wales, R., 28, 34, 50 52
Watson P., 112
White, B.L., 36, 65
Whorf, B.L., 127–8
Wight. J., 135
Woodward, M.W., 35

Yule, W., 123–4

General index

Action programmes, 118
Adjective order, 52–3
Alpern programme, 113
Ambiguous sentences, 57
Animal sounds, 22–3, 24
Anna Karenina, 92
Anxiety, 17, 43
Articulation, 44, 50, 51
Assessment of language difficulty, 3–4, 121
Attention, focussing of, 115
Attention span, 8–9, 43
Auditory behaviour, 39
Auditory discrimination, 115
Authoritarianism, 61, 90–1
Autistic children, 64, 101, 124

Babbling stage, 37, 39
Behaviourist school, 24. 55
Behaviour modification 123–4
Bereiter-Engelmann pre-school project 107–10, 116, 129–30, 138
Blank-Solomon programme, 118–19
Books, 34

Categorizing, 11
Cerebral palsy, 41
Child- adult interaction, 14, 17–21, 31–4, 61–3, 90, 95–6, 112
Child language, early, 31–3
Child-minding, 43
Children in 'care', 66
Choice of language, 47–9, 136–7
Chronological order, 47, 49
Classification, 11, 51, 115
Codes, 76, 77–8, 96
  cultural, 96
  elaborated, 76, 78, 89, 90, 112

159